HEAVEN CAME DOWN

LYNN ANDERSON

THOMAS NELSON PUBLISHERS
Nashville

Published in Nashville, Tennessee, by Thomas Nelson, Inc., Publishers, and distributed in Canada by Word Communications, Ltd., Richmond, British Columbia, and in the United Kingdom by Word (UK), Ltd., Milton Keynes, England.

Library of Congress Cataloging-in-Publication Data

Anderson, Lynn, 1936—
Heaven came down / Lynn Anderson
    p. cm.
Includes bibliographical references.
ISBN 0-8407-4874-4
    1. Jesus Christ—Friends and associates. 2. Interpersonal relations—Religious aspects—Christianity. I. Title.
BT590.F7A53 1993
232.9′5— dc20   93-2548
                                 CIP

Printed in the United States of America

2 3 4 5 6 7 - 98 97 96 95 94

Table of Contents

Acknowledgments

Long years have passed between the conception and the birth of this book. These pages lead through thought-ways which I can trace at least as far back as the 1970s when I fell into my first attempts to mentor college students on people skills. With time the core concepts gathered layers of insight, picked up from dozens of sources which only God knows, as I taught "peopling" seminars across the country. Some ideas may actually be original with me . . . although for the life of me I don't know which ones. Some came from long-time colleagues, with special acknowledgments to Doug Kostowski, Landon Saunders, Stanley Shipp, David Lewis, and David Wray. Some came from the writings of such scholars as the late Donald G. Miller, John Stott, and others.

Some of my former students have taught my material in more than a dozen countries around the globe and have contributed back into the material as well. Among these ex-students is Max Lucado. While in Miami and later in Rio de Janeiro, Max taught this material many times, adding to and adjusting it. While Max was in Brazil, he and I began to collaborate on this book. Max roughed out the first draft from cassettes of sessions I had taught. Then we shuffled manuscripts between Brazil and the U.S. a while. Busy schedules finally stalled the project, and the embryonic manuscript lay in my files for several years.

A publishing deadline with Thomas Nelson finally revived the manuscript some ten months ago. I have reworked the material and added more chapters to bring it to its final form, but if some of this sounds like a young Max Lucado—it is.

To Max, and to all who influenced this book, I am deeply indebted. I pray that Jesus will shine through and leave His mark on those who read it.

Foreword

If you are task-driven but long to be people-oriented—

If you want to see people more as an opportunity than a burden—

If you can't see how the law of God works with the love of God—

If you catch yourself growing irritable at crowds, grumpy at inefficiency, or aggravated at ineptness—

then you are holding the right book.

Lynn Anderson has some words for your heart. He will do more than help you deal with people—he will help you love people. His model? The source of love Himself: Jesus of Nazareth.

Read on and learn how Jesus dealt with difficult people.

— Max Lucado

1

What? Me, Insensitive?

Carolyn and I sat aboard an aircraft in Victoria, British Columbia, ready for departure. From our little oval window we spotted several luggage wagons parked on the tarmac—all piled high with magazines. Every one of those hundreds of magazines bore the same name: *People* magazine! It dawned on us that all over America, millions of people would soon slap down three dollars a throw just to read about the goings-on of other human beings! Amazing, considering that most of us get our fill of people every day.

Then another observation came to my mind. The only real difference between *People* magazine and most other

(It can be cured.)

magazines sold today is the name. Most magazines are about people. *Life* magazine is about people; *Sports Illustrated* is about people; *Time, Newsweek, Popular Mechanics,* even *The Wall Street Journal* are about people. This shouts something about human nature. We are all enormously fascinated with each other. The radio plays songs that are primarily about people; TV is mostly pictures of people. At the movies, we pay good money to sit in the dark to watch shadow pictures of imaginary people. We read novels to get inside the psyches of people. Sometimes, for recreation, we go to the mall to "people watch." Even daily conversation is mostly about *people*. We are driven *by our passion for people*. In fact, our fascination with people is one of the ways in which we are created in the image of God.

Since we are so naturally interested in ourselves and each other, to focus on things, ideas, tasks, status, or institutions does serious damage to the central matrix of our own humanity. Besides, it damages people around us. This came home to me in a very real way just recently.

A coworker had been with us only a few weeks, but something wasn't working right. So I sat down to chat with her a minute, hoping to work through her problem. "Something seems to be bothering you. Can I help?"

I wasn't quite prepared for what I heard next.

"You are plastic!" she said for openers. "You want this place to be user-friendly, but *you* aren't. You are inaccessible and insensitive. You constantly break appointments because you're 'too busy' with what *you* want to do. And you are making the people in this office feel like peons. You are supposed to be a spiritual leader, but I see you as completely unapproachable."

I was stunned. Me? Unapproachable? Insensitive? Surely not me! I tried to deny it, rationalize it, blame everybody else. But . . . really, she was right. Dead right. There was nothing to do but to face it, own it, and apologize to her . . . and, one by one, to the whole staff. And to get back on track.

Yet how had this happened? Didn't I have a reputation for being warm, even sociable? Didn't I have a long and visible track record of good relationships?

But this painful moment of truth forced me to look honestly back at the past many months. Everything was a blur. My pocket calendar was as cluttered as a city dump. Far too many speaking engagements. Way too much travel. Two new books. A new church. Helping launch a new journal. Teaching a graduate course. And page after page of appointments moved or canceled. The pace had gradually accelerated, reaching an all-time high over the last few weeks as I was fighting the contract deadline, ironically, on this book! As my internal engines red-lined, I had become less and less available, more and more self-absorbed.

I am a people-person, but I had allowed myself to become task-driven. For months I had not only been neglecting people, but leaving hurt and disillusioned bodies in my wake, jeopardizing things I really believe to be important.

Because my life was not people-sensitive, it was drifting toward disaster. We are designed to be focused on people, not tasks. To live in community and nurture healthy relationships is to human beings what water is to fish. We were designed for relationships, and without them we lose our humanity.

The Bible says we are designed in the image of God. Our people fascination is our God-likeness. God's number-one priority is people. To do His main thing, God became "a people" and moved to live among people. Jesus, who became "God in a body," was out there on the "people turf."

When Jesus owns us and fills us, we see people in a whole new way. "For Christ's love compels us" and thus we "should no longer live for [our]selves but for him. . . . So from now on we regard no one from a worldly point of view" (2 Cor. 5:14–16). We have a new view of people because "if anyone is in Christ, he is a new creation; the old has gone, the new has come!" (2 Cor. 5:17). The *old view of people* is gone! The *new view of people* has come. And since we are "Christ's ambassadors," God is "making his appeal through us" (2 Cor. 5:20). God has also called us into "people-centered" living. The most "God-like" thing we can do is treat people the way Jesus treats people.

From Abstract to Concrete

When the crowds asked Jesus, "What is the greatest commandment?" He answered, "Love the Lord your God with all your heart and with all your soul and with all your mind and with all your strength" (Mark 12:29–30). That raised no eyebrows and rocked no boats. It was merely the familiar and ancient Shema which bookended all synagogue meetings. It was comfortably abstract. As long as loving God is an abstraction aimed at no target in particular, we are all okay. Ho-hum religion. Business as usual. But then Jesus *added* a line: "Love your neighbor as yourself" (Mark 12:31). Oops! Things changed. Hackles went up. That added line slammed the abstract down onto the concrete. Now Jesus had gone and targeted that teaching. He made it practical. Aimed it at real people.

The way Jesus put it, our love for God is expressed not in pews, pulpits, and stained glass tones, but in relationships among people—in the way you and I get along with him and her and them. If being with God on Sunday doesn't make us better at being with people on Monday, then we missed the point. Real religion shines in right relationships. The grist of Christianity is ground out in the mill of marriages, friendships, partnerships, neighborhoods, communities, property lines, and sales contracts. Or to simplify it, if we really love God, the first ones to know it will be family, friends, and neighbors.

Easier said than done? You better believe it! As the old saying goes,

To live above with those we love,
O, that will be glory.
But to live below with those we know,
Is quite a different story.

As my friend John Chalk says, "It's not just cannibals that get fed up with people!"

The Problem with the World

We come into this world in families; we must fit into society, schools, and other organizations. We must interact with others for success to come to us in any personally effective way (Stephen R. Covey, *Principle-Centered Leadership*). A study a few years back found that 60 to 80 percent of job dismissals in industry were caused by social problems, and only 20 to 40 percent were due to technical incompetence. In other words, most firings were because relationships faltered. The Carnegie Institute showed that in the field of engineering only 15 percent of one's financial success was due to technical knowledge, and 85 percent of one's success was due to one's ability to get along with another person.[1]

Application? Not merely success, but fulfillment—maybe even survival—depends on our ability to manage and nurture healthy relationships.

My, it is hard for us to get along with each other. Linus, the Peanuts comic strip character, said it for all of us, "I love the world. It's *people* that I can't stand." Right, Linus, but doing right by people is still the Christian's forte. Isn't our mission the same as Jesus'? Didn't John say, "For anyone who does not love his brother, whom he has seen, cannot love God, whom he has not seen" (1 John 4:20)?

So we come to an important personal question. *How are your relationships?* Think for just a minute about the people in your world. Some were given to you by choice: your mate, your best friend, perhaps a business associate. Others you got by chance: your relatives, your next-door neighbor, maybe your boss. No matter where you got them, they all have one thing in common. They are people—vulnerable and woundable people—who need someone to love them unreservedly—just like you and I do! And each person matters to God!

Could you use a little help in doing right by people? I guess we all could.

That, in a nutshell, is the purpose of this book: to learn how to treat the people God has put in our world. The plan? Simple. We will track down the way Jesus treated people. And no one marks that way more clearly than the apostle John.

Why John?

Several reasons. John wrote his gospel several decades after the other gospels were written. By this time the church had already begun to form some of the crust of institutionalism. Movements begin flexible and fluid; then they gradually form structure and tradition that help to stabilize them, but also tend to immobilize and desensitize them.

And, worst of all, institutionalized religion tends to become less people-sensitive. In fact, religious institutions can wind up crushing people, even those people who are most Christian. Immobility was already slowing the Christian movement before John died. Bishops were being selected, and organizations were in the early stages of development. Mini-denominations were taking shape. Policies, creeds, and doctrinal statements loomed on the horizon.

The movement was losing people-sensitivity, too. And in the midst of all this sat sensitive Saint John. Wow! Perhaps John's hair was grey and his health frail. All his fellow apostles had long since gone on. No doubt he felt very alone as he faced the changing times. He had witnessed the launching of a movement. Now he watched it languish.

As he surveyed the destruction, his mind may have wandered back to the way things were in the beginning. So spontaneous. So flexible. So full of energy. So relationship-oriented and people-sensitive! Why, the core of Jesus' work had been a three-year relationship with twelve close friends.

John remembered the Messiah solving the wine problem at the wedding, getting the host off the hook. He thought of the blind beggar that no one noticed except Jesus. He reflected upon Jesus' tender teaching of the Samaritan woman, and the tough, direct encounter with Nicodemus. He felt Jesus' tears as He embraced Mary and Martha, consoling them as they mourned for Lazarus. He knew that just as institutions become desensitized, so a crust can form

examples of Jesus' love expressed in actions

around the hearts of individual believers. Relationships can give way to religion, and Christians can lose their "first love."

One can almost hear John thinking aloud. "Jesus was so tender with people, yet so tough with issues. Jesus and people. That is it! That has to be remembered."

So John wrote it down. "These are written that you may believe that Jesus is the Christ, the Son of God, and that by believing you may have life in his name" (John 20:31). In other words, "I want to build your faith!" High-powered theology in human interest stories. Stories about people. Stories about relationships. Ordinary encounter after ordinary encounter. Each story carefully selected to weave a tapestry of ageless wisdom. Heaven touching humanity, Immanuel among earthlings, the Christ amidst the commoners, *Jesus and people.*

With graphic detail and penetrating insight, John takes us on a storybook journey through Jesus' encounters with human beings. All kinds of people:

- religious people like Nicodemus
- righteous people like the Pharisees
- abandoned people like the woman at the well
- frightened people like the woman caught in adultery
- despairing people like Mary and Martha at the tomb of Lazarus
- lonely people like the man by the pool
- mistreated people like the blind beggar by the road

And the common thread that strings these souls together is their basic humanity. They had flesh and bones, problems and joys, friends and enemies. Like you and me!

They could have been your neighbors or your relatives. That cranky old coot that lives around the corner? He is in John's story. That group of church officials who can't see God? Jesus ran into a few of those. The pregnant teenager? The grief-stricken widow? You'll see their faces on the pages of John's writings. And, what's more, Jesus is one of them, yet in Him you'll see God act out His own commandment. You'll watch Him love them as He loved Himself, and you'll want to love like that! You will observe divine people skills, and you can learn them. You will see that God does His most awesome work through relationships. Hopefully, with a touch from beyond, your own relationships will be changed!

At a baptismal service, one of our friends was explaining to her three-year-old daughter the significance of what they were witnessing. "See that lady?" the mother asked. "Jesus is about to wash away her sins."

The little girl sat up a bit straighter so she could see better and said with excitement, "Good, I've been wanting to see Jesus."

Me, too, little one. I have, too!

Maybe you have, too. Maybe you have heard Jesus' words about loving your neighbor as yourself and have thought, "I'd like to see what He would do with that in my world!" Well, now is your chance. Let's open our hearts a bit and let John teach us how Jesus treated people.

When John raised his bony finger and exploded, "That's Him!" we couldn't believe our eyes. Goodness knows we'd heard enough about Him. He was all John talked about. Rumors about Him roamed the countryside. Strange things. Lights moving through the sky. Other-worldly choir music at night out in the country. Disturbing ideas. Miracles?

Now, here He was on our street. John spotted Him in the next block headed our way. You could have knocked me over with a feather. We watched bug-eyed and held our breath while He walked by. Yet frankly, part of me was a bit disappointed. He was so . . . uh . . . ordinary. Looked pretty much like any other Galilean carpenter.

James and I let Him get a few strides past, then fell in behind Him. I'm not sure why. It seems sort of dumb now as I look back. Then, without warning, He turned around and spoke to us. I was so rattled that I didn't really hear what He said. James told me later He asked us a simple question, "You fellows looking for something?" I stammered back, "Uh . . . where do you live?" Silly question, but it was all I could come up with. Yet somehow His answer made me feel as if mine was the most appropriate question in the world—as if God had planned for centuries that I should ask exactly that.

His eyes twinkled with a warm light. And He said, "Come and see!"

We followed Him home that day . . . been following ever since.

2

Street-Level Messiah

Four principles. Like four legs on a chair—a balanced place to rest one's convictions. Like four walls in a room—a shelter from the chill of cold people and a shade from the blistering heat of hotheads. Four solid traits. Four tools found in the Master's tool chest for building relationships with people.

Over and over these four principles weave in and out of the gospels, creating a tapestry of four colors. Each blending with the other. Each creating the other. Each supporting the other.

Yet each, unique. Common in purpose, but different in function. Alone each helps us, but together they can trans-

Of Lovers and Users

form us. They were designed in heaven for use on earth. Four basic peopling principles:

- Jesus was *available.*
- Jesus was *sensitive.*
- Jesus was *helpful.*
- Jesus was *creative.*

Available

Let's take them from the top. Principle number one: Jesus was *available* to people. John makes this clear up front. "The Word became flesh and lived for a while among us" (John 1:14). Although Jesus was *with* God, He *was* God, and He made everything; He "became flesh." He pitched His tent right smack in the middle of our campground; He rented a house on your block and walked down my street. Let's follow Jesus as He walks into His first conversation in the gospel of John.

A young prophet and a few of his friends are standing in an ancient village street. "John [the Baptist] saw Jesus coming toward him" (John 1:29). That's street-level availability. There Jesus was on the street walking toward John the Baptizer and two friends. Physically accessible.

The two disciples fell in behind Jesus and followed Him. Sensing them behind Him, Jesus turned on His heel and asked, "What do you want?"

They met His question with another question, "Where are you staying?"

"Come," He replied, "and you will see." So they went and saw where He was staying and they spent the day with Him. Jesus is not hiding out somewhere in an office, running a rigid schedule that allows no time for people. But He's with the people, and He made His whole day available to these seekers. (I wish I knew what He knows without having to hide in the office to learn it.) What's more, Jesus wasn't merely geographically present, but He was *emotionally* available to people as well. He was approachable. People could walk up and talk to Him, ask Him questions, carry on conversations. Sometimes when He was teaching His disciples they interrupted Him in the middle of His sermons, and He didn't seem to mind at all. In fact, that's how He wanted it.

What are the implications for me? If I am going to follow Jesus' lead, I will be available to people. I need to be where the people are. And not just physically near, but personally approachable. As my coworker so courageously but kindly pointed out to me, there is something both askew and less than credible about a person who professes to be spiritually alive but is personally unapproachable. Amen and ouch!

Sensitive

Principle number two: *Jesus was sensitive.* Jesus was tuned in. He picked up on subtle people signals. John notices this early in his gospel. Watch as John the Baptizer pointed out Jesus walking down the street and John's disciples fell in behind Jesus. What does a person do when he suddenly notices people following him? He either quickens the pace or turns and confronts. Right? Jesus turned and faced these curious followers, but not so much in confrontation as in user-friendly dialogue.

Sensitive to their presence, He felt someone following Him, yes. He wasn't hidden away in His own contemplative ivory tower. He walked in the real world, aware of people following Him. But on a deeper level, Jesus sensed some of *why* they were following. When Jesus turned He perceptively inquired, "What do you want?" or was it, "What can I do for you?"

When you are following someone who suddenly wheels around and speaks to you, how do you respond? You feel obligated to explain what you are up to, right? And likely, at first, you will be at a loss for words. Seems the disciples were, too. They respond, "Uh . . . uh . . . where do you live?" What else could they say? Jesus, still sensitive, first to their quest, but now to their feelings of awkwardness, replied, "Come and see." He could have squelched their "Where do you live?" with "That's a dumb question. I don't live any place. Foxes have holes. I don't have a place to lay My head." But Jesus gently probed, "Come and see."

Jesus wasn't saying, "I'm over at the Hilton, room 326. Come and look at the place." No, I think Jesus meant, "Come with Me and I will show you something about the perspective from which I live My life. Come and I'll show you the wonderful world of the Spirit."

He will always be sensitive. Later in this same chapter of John's gospel, Jesus introduced Nathanael. He said, "Here is a true Israelite, in whom there is nothing false" (John 1:47).

"How do you know me?" Nathanael asked.

"When you were over there under the fig tree," Jesus explained, "before Philip even called you, *I saw you.*" More than mechanics is conveyed here. He doesn't mean merely, "A beam of light struck you and bounced onto My optic nerve, transferring your image to My brain." Rather, Jesus *perceived* something about Nathanael. Jesus is sensitive. This leaves me asking, "Am I the kind of person who picks up on the subtle signals people send?" If not, why? *Honestly,* why? And if so, why?

After all, two kinds of characters are people-sensi-tive: the lovers and the users. Some people have learned to read subtle signals because they are lov-ers. They care about people, so they study people all the time. Love makes us sensitive to people.

But "users" become sensitive to people-signals for a very different purpose. The hawkers at the circus sideshow can read people like a book. They know how to manipulate. Fortune-tellers ask leading questions, probe here and there, and pick up on clothing, facial expression, body language. But they are people-sen-sitive because they're *users*.

Of course, Jesus was a *lover*, not a *user!* His followers will become skillful lovers as well. This means being alert to the environment, keeping your head in the game. Someone has said, "If you are not completely where you are wherever you are, then you are nowhere."

Of course, "God has poured out his love into our hearts by the Holy Spirit" (Rom. 5:5). The Spirit within us is the fountain source of people-sensitiveness. But Christians can help each other learn sensitivity, too. Especially, parents can help children. When our children were small, Carolyn and I defined five quali-ties we wanted to nurture in our kids.

First, and foremost, we wanted them to love God.

Second, we wanted them to develop healthy self-es-teem; third, to be self-starters; fourth, to manage healthy relationships. Finally, we wanted our chil-dren to be people-sensitive. We knew that we had to role model people-sensitiveness. But we also tried all sorts of strategies to "people-sensitize" our kids. One effective strategy was a little game we played with them in parks, malls, airports, or any other good place for people-watching. We would pick out some interesting by-passer and challenge the kids to make up a story about that person. But they had to give reasons their stories could be true. "That man over there is very lonely. He looks sad. Last night while he was sleeping alone on a park bench, he. . . ."

"Why do you think he slept on a park bench?"

"Because his clothes are wrinkled, he looks poor, and he needs a shave. And you can smell that he didn't get a shower this morning. . . ."

The kids would go on watching for clues, making up stories about strangers . . . and in so doing, sharpening their powers of observation, deepening their hearts, and refining their people-sensitivity. We believe God blessed those games.

Helpful

Principle number three: Jesus was also *helpful.* Some folks are only superficially available and kind. Bleeding hearts. They wring their hands and whine, "Ain't it awful, what's happening to So-and-so?" Or "Oh, I feel so deeply for people that I just can't stand to go into a hospital room because I get sick myself out of empathy; I'm so tenderhearted." Or, "I can't comfort the bereaved because grief absolutely devastates me." That's not people-sensitive! That's *self-*sensitive. People-sensitivity looks for a way to help. Self-sensitivity ducks unpleasant experiences, even if this means neglecting sick, brokenhearted people. Real sensitivity pays the cost of getting involved. It's so simple you'd think everyone would naturally be helpful. Not always.

I read about a woman shopping in a major metropolis who fell and broke her leg. She sat helpless, crying, calling for someone to be kind enough to help her. How long would you guess she cried? Two minutes? Ten minutes? Twenty minutes? Keep guessing.

This woman pleaded for *forty* minutes as people walked on by before someone stopped and actually *helped* her!

If we could interview those who walked around and stepped over that woman, we might be surprised. Would some be civic leaders? Businesspersons? Would some be Christians? How am I on the helpfulness chart? How is your track record of kindness? Let's think about our friends. Is there someone who could use our help?

- That colleague at work who has more assignments than he can possibly get done.
- That young mother down the street whose day is framed with baby food and diapers.
- The teenager who has no parent to pick him or her up after school.
- The elderly woman who may need a strong back to help her move some furniture.

Helpfulness is the bread and butter of the Christian virtues. It should be "standard equipment" on all models. Not all can preach. Few can lead. Not everyone is a musician or can counsel or teach. But all *can* be *helpful.* Anyone can roll up his or her pants legs and wade into the flood of day-to-day hassles and hurts of others. And to do this is to do what Jesus did; it is, in fact, to be *like God!*

Now look back at Jesus! The first question He asked John's disciples who were soft-shoeing along behind Him was, "What can I do for you? Is there something I can do to help?" Jesus' question was not a challenge, "What are you guys after?" but helpful empathy, "Is there something I can help you with?"

"Yes, there is," they said. "We want to know where You live."

He said, "All right, fine, I can *help* you with that. Come on and I'll show you." Now, His agenda wasn't what they expected. But my, was He helpful! A helping person is a Jesus person.

Creative

Availability. Sensitivity. Helpfulness. Quite a trio. But let's unveil the fourth and most exciting feature in Jesus' style! Jesus was *creative*.

A friend pointed out that God has a thing about "differentness" and "variety." God created 300,000 species of beetles. In a cubic foot of snow, there are 18 million individual crystals, and not one of them is like any of the others. God only makes originals. Doesn't allow copies. Breaks every mold He uses. This creative genius reaches its crescendo in human beings. We are "fearfully and wonderfully made" (Ps. 139:14). God's grace is so many-colored that He cannot express Himself in only one kind of human being.

Look away from this page for a moment. Examine the tips of your fingers. Use a magnifying glass if you need to, and study your fingerprints. Each fingerprint is unique. No two are alike. That's how the cops track down criminals. Yours are different from any other fingerprints in the whole wide world, maybe the only ones exactly like this that have ever existed! How wonderful! The God who went to the trouble to design uniqueness on our fingertips didn't stop there.

The God who makes one-of-a-kind fingerprints graciously puts them on the end of one-of-a-kind persons as well. Our uniqueness runs up our arms and into our whole bodies, into our whole emotional histories, into our priceless one-of-a-kind original souls!

And since God has made each person uniquely different, Jesus creatively deals with every person in a fresh, unique way.

Begin with a Question

Jesus did not manipulate people, nor should we. In fact, as we track Jesus, we are not looking for techniques. God Himself in flesh stands in awe of the sacredness and dignity of human personality. He doesn't employ pressure tactics to batter down the walls of people's hearts or bulldoze His way into the sanctity of their spirits. Instead, He approaches each one carefully, creatively. The first example John reports of Jesus' creative approach to people is *the importance of questions.* Jesus opens His first encounter with a question.

All through His ministry, Jesus will ask questions: "Will you give me a drink?" (John 4:7) "Do you want to get well?" (John 5:6) "You do not want to leave too, do you?" (John 6:67) "Do you believe in the Son of Man?" (John 9:35) "I am the resurrection and the life. . . . Do you believe this?" (John 11:25–26) "John's baptism—where did it come from? Was it from heaven, or from men?" (Matt. 21:25) Jesus begins relationships, grants dignity to people, even opens up closed minds with simple questions.

We religious types often seem more inclined toward telling than asking. But most people like to be asked before they are told. Jesus sees people as too valuable to simply "get them told." He sees them as free and capable to do their own responding. So He just asks questions and lets each person think. Modern educators find this to be a sound educational principle. It's also a wonderful and welcomed conversational style.

One day back in 1971, I boarded a plane in Abilene, Texas, and settled in beside a twenty-year-old young man who appeared incredibly nervous. Assuming he feared flying, I asked, "Do you fly much?"

He explained that he was no white-knuckle novice, that he flew all the time. Then he added, "Why do you ask?"

I explained, "You seemed to be a little nervous and I thought maybe—"

"No, no," he said, "that's not it at all. I *am* pretty nervous all right. But it's because I'm on my way to Vietnam."

What would you say next? I lost my bearings but stumbled on, "Oh, uh, well, er, how long do you expect to be over there?"

A long silence preceded the next words, "I don't expect to come back."

Shocked, I waited a few nervous moments, then probed, "Tell me about it."

"Three of my high school friends are never coming back. Well, they came back all right—in a box. Man, I really don't expect to come back alive either."

Tears filled his eyes. Silence. Then I observed, "That's a tough thing to face. Do you have any idea how you're going to deal with all of that?"

"Oh, yeah," his face brightened.

I thought maybe he was a bright-eyed, bushy-tailed born-again seminary student and was getting ready to lay his testimony on me. I leaned in.

"Well, I'm going to save up all my money so that just in case I ever do get back on American soil again, I'll be able to buy a brand new purple motorcycle. I'll just live for that day!"

Four simple questions! Actually, four important and innocent questions. I had no strategy in mind when I asked them. But those small questions not

only opened up this young man's universe and sur-
faced the terror buried in his soul, but also measured
his flimsy resources for coping with such overwhelm-
ing possibilities. I don't think he felt he had been
intruded upon at all.

On another occasion I found myself in a strange
conversation that could have gone a lot better with
one or two well-placed questions. Carolyn and I sat
by a hotel pool when an interesting couple walked by
with their children. A New Testament stuck out of the
back pocket of the man's blue jeans, which were
pulled down neatly over his cowboy boots and rolled
up one turn at the bottom.

Something inside me said, "This guy has got to be
religious; he might even be clergy." So I engaged him
in conversation.

"Do you farm near here?"

"No," he explained, "I preach the gospel."

Some strange quirk in my nature chose not to
reveal who I was. So for an hour or more I pretended
to be an "evangelistic prospect." In fact, I never did
tell the couple who I was or what I did, mostly because
he never asked. In fact, he never *asked* me anything.
He merely *told*. I inquired, "Oh, what kind of
preacher?"

"Well, what kind is there? I preach Jesus, like in
the New Testament."

"What is the New Testament?"

"Second part of the Bible. First there is the Old
Testament and then the New Testament."

"So you don't believe in the Old Testament?"

"Well, not exactly. . . ."

He held forth a while on dispensationalism and
Hebrew versus Greek manuscripts, etc. I couldn't
resist the temptation to push things further.

"At what seminary did you get your rabbi's degree?"

"I'm not a rabbi, I'm a *Christian* minister."

"What kind of church?"

"The kind that Jesus started on the day of Pentecost."

"The day of *what?*"

"It was a Jewish holiday."

"Oh, so you are a Jewish preacher?"

Although he was very patient with me and eager to answer my questions, he didn't seem even remotely interested in me as a person. He just led me on a survey of theology, church history, the plan of salvation, "true worship," all orthodox Christianity, I suppose. However, if he had only asked one or two questions about me, he would have made the whole conversation unnecessary.

If, on the other hand, I had been who this man thought I was, I would scarcely have understood a word he was saying. The weird religious jargon would have killed any interest that I might have brought to the encounter. And I certainly would not have connected any of his abstractions with my life.

Now, the reason I remember that encounter so clearly is that I have been on his end of this conversation a thousand times. I feel pained when I think how many sincere people I have turned off, not necessarily because my message was wrong, but because I started in the wrong place. I didn't ask enough of the right questions. I was more interested in telling than in listening. How many people may have tried, but simply couldn't decode my message? How many would love to know God if only they could peel away the layers of religious packaging I wrapped around it? How many felt regarded as *prospects* rather than *persons?* Oh, yes, a few well-placed questions could have made all the difference!

Questions must be carefully chosen and delicately worded, however, or they can be fists hammering on the doors of personal privacy. Have you ever been questioned—rat-ta-tat-ta-tat, and you felt as if someone were breaking and entering your psyche? You wanted to run. When Jesus confronted John's disciples, He did not cross-examine them. He never does that. His questions are always sensitive. Often indirect. *Person-oriented, not agenda-oriented.*

Nor were Jesus' questions manipulative, like the kind salespersons sometimes use—cleverly sequenced so that whatever you answer, the sales rep will pick up on your response and lead you to another crossroads where he nails you with another leading question. Several years ago when one salesman came to our house, Carolyn and I pre-planned that no matter what he said, neither of us would say a word.

He walked in. I greeted him with a fixed smile. He spoke a few sentences then asked a question.

We just smiled at him. He waited. We kept smiling (and squirming). The salesman shifted directions, to another crossroads, then stopped and asked another question. We just kept smiling. After a half a dozen questions, the salesman gathered up his papers, threw them into his briefcase, and headed out the door muttering to himself.

I'm not suggesting that every salesperson is a manipulator, nor am I recommending the silent treatment for all hard-working salespersons. I'm saying that Jesus didn't use manipulative questions. His are genuine concern questions; the kind of questions that pulled Him up alongside people, gently opening hearts, yet letting the comfort zone of the other person dictate the pace.

"The Word became flesh and lived for a while among us"; thus, we "have seen his glory," says John (John

1:14). Available. Sensitive. Helpful. Creative. And if
we follow Jesus, He delegates that role to us. Wow!
So we become "God expressed in human form" on the
street where we live. Incredible! And now we have
become "Christ's ambassadors, as though God were
making his appeal through us" (2 Cor. 5:20). That
means that we, His followers, will want to treat others
as Jesus would treat them. And here, in Jesus'
encounter with the disciples of John, we find creative
key number one: *Questions.* One God-like, people-
sensitive quality is the art of gentle, well-chosen
questions. Let's learn. Turn the page and look for
more creative Christ-like keys to healthy human
relationships.

Focus:

1. In what ways are you approachable?
2. What kind of insights are necessary to be sensitive?
3. How would a person cultivate sensitivity and ap-
   proachability?
4. Is there a person with needs who has been reaching out to you, but you have avoided the opportunity? How does this chapter convict you to
   act differently? How would Jesus act?
5. As an experiment, in your next conversation with
   a friend, try asking questions. Try to genuinely
   show that you're interested in that friend.

*P*anic on the servants' faces signaled that something was going wrong at my daughter's wedding. Then the maître d' slipped up and whispered in my ear, "Master, we've run out of wine."

My mouth went dry, and my stomach knotted. This can't be happening to me. And I've ruined the biggest day in the life of my sweet, trusting daughter.

I may even have ruined myself! Everyone knows that a wedding invitation for distant travellers implies that I will provide everything for them—lodging and food and music and dancing—and, of course, wine. Our courts regard an invitation like ours as a legal contract. Rumor has it that when Ben Enoch, over in Capernaum, ran out of wine at his daughter's wedding, poor Ben was hit with a half-dozen lawsuits—destroyed him financially.

Why am I running short of wine? Maybe because that country carpenter brought His twelve uninvited extras. Look, His mother is whispering something to Him; I hope it's a tongue-lashing on protocol. What? The nerve of this guy! He just called for more to drink!

Did He say "water"? All that water! Wait a minute . . . would you believe? . . .

Well, young John may have told you what happened next. . . . Oh yes, it's true. True. But given who He is it's the last thing I would have expected. Surely He might have done something . . . well . . . something more like God! Maybe chided me for carelessness, or even have stepped up on the table and delivered a synagogue-scorching sermon on "Wine is a mocker." But no. It seems my feelings mattered to Him far more than my blunders.

I agree with His twelve friends. They said they saw God's glory that day. Glory? God the miraculous winemaker? No! Glory! God who begins with our feelings, not our failures; who cares more about our hearts than our history. Who besides God?

3

The Wine of Kindness

The plot seems too simple. Jesus and His disciples visit a wedding. The host runs out of wine. Apparently, the wine shop is closed. So Jesus turns six jugs of water into six jugs of wine! Simple, huh? But what is this story doing in the Bible? The conclusion seems so open-ended. And, without question, this story has triggered a thousand arguments over wine drinking and Christian temperance. Where is the meat in this story? The action? The depth?

This story certainly doesn't swing the kind of clout wielded by the account of Jesus' calling Lazarus from the

(or Helping a Host Off the Hook)

tomb. It's not as dramatic as running the money-changers out of the temple.

Or is it?

Wait! A second look may explain why John dropped this drama in as one of his lead-off numbers. Actually, it is one of the richest stories in the gospel. Not only does it set the tone for Jesus' dealings with people, it embodies His principal attitude toward human beings. He starts where they are!

But before we jump into the story, it might be wise to clarify a couple of things. First, the "water to wine" story was *not* intended to cast a vote on booze. Some people fasten onto this text to support a little "tip of the bottle" now and then. That is not what the story is about. And to reduce it to that level is to miss the point entirely.

Some over-spiritualize the passage. For example: "The water of the law is replaced by the wine of the Spirit." Or, "Not the water of ritual, but the wine of a relationship." Or, "Once the water of legalism, now the wine of grace." Good ideas! But not the point of Jesus' wedding wine.

Actually, Jesus gives us a very practical lesson on kindness. God responds to the most "human" of problems: social embarrassment. And He *starts with people where they are!*

He Showed Up

Don't miss something subtle but striking in this story: the simple fact that Jesus showed up at a wedding. In other words, Jesus (God) is very much *available* to people. He is involved in the normal processes of human living. Besides, weddings are celebrations, which means that Jesus was available at a place where people were *celebrating*. Deity descended and partied with people! Some people seem to think Christians are supposed to wear a sign that says, "No fun, no sun, and no laughs." They're the dreary crowd with solemn faces and sourpuss expressions, who spend long nights at home. The "really spiritual" Christian knows how to turn down invitations, turn up his nose at jokes, and turn his back on anything that seems to suggest a good time.

Obviously, this is not so with Jesus. The simple fact that He was *invited* to the wedding suggests that people enjoyed being around Jesus and that He enjoyed being with people. He was likeable. Approachable. Huggable. He knew how to listen. Doubtless, He knew how to throw back His head and flood a room with laughter. His Father's love made Him *connect* with people, not *dodge* them. Jesus was a life-lover and a life-giver to the fullest. He said in John 10:10, "I have come that they may have life, and have it to the full." Note these wise words of Charles Spurgeon:

> Sing, Christian, wherever you go; try, if you can, to wash your face every morning in a bath of praise. When you go down from your chamber, never go to look on men till you have first looked on your God; and when you have looked on him, seek to come down with a face beaming with joy; carry a smile, for you will cheer up many a poor way-worn pilgrim by it.[2]

If anyone has reason to enjoy life, surely Christians do. Who else stands on such solid security? Or trusts in such promises? Or expects such a bright tomorrow? A Christian carries a key to eternity! If that doesn't make him want to get out and rub elbows with neighbors at a picnic or join in the city parade or sing in the local glee club, then something is off-target.

He Knew What Was Going On

This piece of Scripture does not specifically state that Jesus was *sensitive*, but again that voice between the lines shouts sensitivity.

Weddings back then and over there differed a bit from here and now nuptials. For one thing, those weddings usually lasted several days. Guests and family would gather at sundown with the bride and groom for a long, candlelight procession to the couple's home. The entourage would wind through the soft evening twilight of the narrow city streets, singing and celebrating. In the gathering darkness, candlelight and joy glowed in the happy faces. After the ceremony, instead of a honeymoon trip, the bride and groom would stay at the home for several days, reigning like a king and queen.

There was gift-giving, speech-making, food-eating, and, you guessed it, lots of wine-drinking. Gifts, food, and wine were matters of high protocol. The food was to be well-prepared. The wine flowed in abundance. And if you showed up with an inappropriate gift, the bride and groom could bar you permanently from polite circles.

Worse yet, if you wanted to be a humiliated host, just run short on food or wine. Jesus knew that was not merely an embarrassing little bobble in the kitchen. Oh, no! It was absolutely unthinkable. A total disgrace to the family. After all, folks had come from great distances to answer your invitation. And what with no McDonald's, no 7–11, no Visa, or American Express, the guests were totally dependent on their host. These social customs were taken so seriously that guests could actually bring a lawsuit if they were not properly cared for. So, when Mary took Jesus off to one side and whispered, "They have no more wine," she sounded more than a mild note of alarm.

At first glance, it may appear that Jesus was reluctant to help. "Dear woman, why do you involve me? My time has not yet come," He responded (John 2:4).

Jesus appears to follow a clear time line. His life was not lived out in a vague cloud of random "happenings." He moved toward a purpose, working according to God's timetable.

However, Jesus was facing conflict between the plans on the divine calendar and the human needs of the hour. This surprise emergency was disturbing a well-laid agenda and disrupting a comfortable pace.

In our day of computers, Day-Timers, and time management, there isn't much room left over for sudden shifts in plans. The sacredness of our airtight schedules can squeeze out space for spontaneous response to the people who pop up in our paths. Examples?

- The one who cuts short the phone call from a discouraged friend because it might make him late for a meeting of the "Compassion Committee."
- The preacher who defers responding to the grief of the church member because it's Wednesday and everyone knows that Wednesday is for sermon preparation.
- The father who is too busy *providing* for his family to take a day off to *love* his family.
- The mom who doesn't have time to listen to her teenager's life-pivotal question because she's got to clean the house.

You may be furrowing your brow in disagreement. "But what is wrong with a meeting on compassion?" Or "Shouldn't a minister study?" And "Is there some virtue in a sloppy house?" The answers are "nothing," "yes," and "no." But we have to remember that these are *means* to ends and not the ends themselves.

There is nothing inherently holy in a "Compassion Committee," especially if that meeting keeps us away from people. A preacher who will ignore a hurting flock will find little credibility for his well-crafted sermon. And parents who neglect relationship with family in order to clean houses and pay bills are only kidding themselves about "caring for their families."

Now, please don't miss the point. We need disciplined schedules. Good things don't happen without good plans, and good plans don't get worked without disciplined schedules. But when plans push aside people, isn't something off balance?

This imbalance hit ridiculous extremes early one Sunday morning. Ed, a staff associate in our church, had downed his last swallow of coffee and picked up his coat, ready to head for work when he heard loud pounding on his front door. When the door swung open, Mary, from two doors down, burst into the living room. Utter panic blanched her face and distorted her voice. Just minutes earlier, Frank, Mary's husband, had fallen, crashed through a glass windowpane, and cut himself horribly. He was spurt-bleeding and in deep trouble. Mary had to get to the emergency room—now! Time was running out.

Mary's panic had shot off the charts when she had first knocked on the door of the neighbors between her house and Ed's. The neighbors had politely expressed their empathy with Frank's and Mary's situation, said they felt badly that they could do nothing. But, with solemn "spiritual" expressions on their faces, had explained, "We would really like to help you. But we are late to church." They had "never forsaken the house of God on the Lord's day in years," not for any reason. God comes first. Surely Mary would respect that and understand.

This story is incredible—but unfortunately, it is also true. And, of course, it could not be further from the heart of Jesus. Oh, no. For Jesus: *Sensitivity mandates that we let our actions be determined just as much by the needs of people as by events on a calendar.*

That's what happened at the wedding. Jesus was headed toward "His hour." But God was saying, "Be sensitive to these people. Be responsive to their needs." They were His friends, and He felt their critical dilemma. So He shifted His plans. But this is not the only time; He did this also when the woman with the chronic hemorrhage touched Jesus as He was on His way to the bedside of a dying girl, and when He greeted a Samaritan woman at a well.

But then, at other times Jesus clearly chose *not* to change His plans even in the face of what seemed to be legitimate and urgent needs. For example, when Jesus got word that His friend Lazarus was dying, instead of rushing to help, Jesus stayed "where he was two more days" (John 11:6).

How did Jesus know when to flow to the emergency and when to stick to His calendar? Divine insight may have played a part, of course, but a couple of practical pointers pop up here. The next time the plans on your calendar conflict with the needs of the hour, ask yourself these two questions.

First, is it a true emergency? Jesus was willing to change when the emergency was a true emergency. The wedding host had his back to the wall. Wine *had* to be provided, or disaster could befall the family.

Many apparent emergencies in reality turn out to be long-standing problems dressed in the red flags of panic. Jesus may be prompting us here to differentiate between the true crisis and the ongoing problem, which may be serious, but not immediately critical.

Late one Friday night, a panic phone call wakened my friend Ron.

"Ron, it's Mac. You gotta come talk to us right away. Barbara is threatening to leave me."

My friend Ron is the kind of guy who is always willing to go out of his way to help. But this time he was due to leave before dawn on business and wouldn't be back till the next Wednesday.

"Mac, how long have you and Barbara been having problems?"

"Actually, Ron, ever since we've been married, five years."

"Mac. It's very unlikely that one midnight conversation is going to fix a problem that has been brewing for years. How'd it be if I meet with you and Barb next Thursday? Things will have cooled down, and we'll have more time to talk. Besides, my flight leaves at—"

"But, Ron, Thursday is five days off. Something might come up—"

"Just write it on your calendar. Don't schedule anything else."

"C'mon, Ron, who knows what we will be doing five days from now. . . ."

Ron didn't go. This was not an emergency. If he had gone he would not have helped Mac and Barbara. In fact, he would have reinforced Mac's habit of irresponsibility. By Thursday, Mac forgot "his problem." Ron did the right thing.

A second question to ask: Is there anyone else who can and should meet this need? In this case, only Jesus could meet the need. Most needs can be met by any number of people. Yet a few are tailor-made for you. For me, too! Maybe you have had personal experiences with problems similar to the specific problem at hand. Or maybe I am closer to a certain troubled person than anyone else. There are times when only you can meet a person's need. At those times, the Spirit may be leading you to be flexible, to shift your plans, or to scrap your agenda.

May I Help You?

When the host ran out of wine, Jesus did something about it. "Bring me the water jars." They brought six stone jars, each containing twenty or thirty gallons of water. Something big was about to happen! Something that couldn't be ignored. Boom! Jesus instantly made more than 120 gallons of wine.

Jesus is being *helpful*. The availability and sensitivity of Jesus would have been useless had He not been willing to meet a practical need. He didn't cop out by saying, "I'm sent here to preach, not to turn water into wine. Besides, if I make all this wine, I'll trigger arguments in Bible study groups from now till the end of time!" No, Jesus saw a person in a tight spot and knew that only He could help. So He did! Simple as that.

Not just available this time. Not merely sensitive. But, oh so *helpful*. The host got off the hook, the bride got blessed, and the ruler of the feast got a reprieve—all because of what Jesus did.

Let's watch that: available, sensitive, and helpful—and creative.

A One-of-a-Kind Original

Yes! Jesus was ever so *creative*, the most beautiful principle of all! Remember, He never treated two people the same way. No "one-size-fits-all" approach to human problems. No franchised procedures, indexed to cover all categories: method one, drunks; method two, businesspersons; method three, homemakers. Jesus didn't see people as units to be run through some canned spiel or process. He saw each person as magnificently special!

To categorize persons is to squelch their personhood and to slam our Father's creative grace. Not Jesus. He is creative! Since each person is unique, from our fingerprints to our hair follicles, each person is to be treated as special.

And Jesus creatively *begins where we are*. He met this man at the point of felt need—without immediate approval or disapproval being implied.

Now, what *is* a "felt need"? Contrast "felt" and "central" needs. The central human need is spiritual. People are separated from God, alienated because of sin, needing a relationship with Him. The chaos in their lives, the things that go wrong, can be traced back to the need for God. True. But the symptoms are "felt" needs. People *feel* lonely, or *feel* they don't have enough money, or are married to the wrong person, or are too fat or too skinny or too tall or too short, or work the wrong job, or serve the wrong boss, or have acne, or whatever! They perceive the surface problem as "the" problem. This surface problem is their "felt" need. Although the real need is spiritual, we cannot bypass felt needs, ignore "feelings," and shove persons directly into "God-talk."

That didn't work for Ned. Ned is a bashful barber who felt convicted by his pastor's series on witnessing. He got a man in his chair, lathered him with shaving cream, brandished his razor, and nervously blurted, "Are you prepared to meet your God?" We may admire the zeal, but the man in the chair got the wrong message!

Jon, our oldest son, played Little League with a kid we'll call Timmy. Timmy's mother was a health food nut. (Oops! Carolyn keeps reminding me to say, "She was fascinated with nutrition.") Timmy's mother believed that most problems—from emotional upsets to lack of coordination to insomnia—could be traced to a potassium deficiency. Everybody knows where potassium comes from. Bananas, right?

So, one day at practice, Jon was fighting a three-game batting slump, muttering to himself, "Dad says that I'm taking my eye off the ball." Timmy got up in Jon's face and said, "Have you tried bananas?" Jon threw a bewildered glance at Timmy, then further theorized, "Maybe I'm swinging too late."

Timmy gushed, "Bananas. Have you ever tried bananas with honey and peanut butter?"

Jon backed away, shaking his head, and walked over to me, "Dad, that guy Timmy is *bananas*."

But suppose Timmy's mother was right, that Jon's coordination was off because of potassium deficiency and he needed to eat more bananas. Jon's *felt* need was a batting slump. His *real need* may have been bananas. But Jon saw absolutely no connection between bananas and batting slumps. So Timmy made no sense to him.

Here at Cana, Jesus met a "felt need" in a uniquely creative way. Yes, He could have seized the opportunity for a scathing sermon on the evils of alcohol abuse. Look at the stage props—six stone jars and possibly a dozen drunks.

But Jesus didn't do that. It was not the right people time. Wine was not the point here. People were. And Jesus dealt with persons, not issues. He made some wine in order that somehow His glory would be seen. Was the glory in the miracle? No, His glory is revealed in that He sees and feels the needs of real people. Now, that's glorious! God cares about people! And we can reflect His glory by doing the same.

Jesus does not operate like one visiting evangelist who preached a revival at a country church of my student ministry days. After months of relationship-building, a lady who didn't know God and didn't trust churches finally consented to attend our church during our revival. As she stepped from her car in front of the church, she took one last drag on her cigarette. To the shock of all who stood nearby, the visiting evangelist grabbed the cigarette from her mouth, threw it on the ground, and verbally ripped into her, "Smoking dishonors God and rots your lungs and yellows your fingertips!" She looked horri-fied, stormed into her car, and roared off the lot. Needless to say, she has never darkened the church doorway since. That woman didn't need a diatribe on smoking. She needed Jesus.

Jesus treats people more like some college stu-dents treated a lady we'll call Rachel. They met Rachel while working in a summer intern program in Miami, Florida. Rachel was sobbing hysterically on a resi-dential sidewalk. She worked for a funeral home and had just accidently switched two urns of ashes and delivered them to the wrong families. The poor woman panicked, "What am I going to do? I've just watched Lois grieve *again* over Harry's ashes, but they were really Tom's. How can I go back and say, 'Whoops, you got Tom. This jar is Harry'?" Rather than laugh at her or shame her for such carelessness, the students contrived an ingenious plan to secretly switch the urns. In this way, they met Rachel's felt need. In retrospect, we may see the situation as funny, but it didn't look that way at the time, at least not to Rachel. Through that need-meeting, the students developed a relationship with Rachel and eventually led her to Christ. In this way, her *real* need was met as well, even though they began with her *felt* need.

The same summer, the students met "Bill," an alcoholic. They found him collapsed on the street in delirium tremors from alcohol withdrawal. One of the students, recognizing the syndrome, rushed across the street to the convenience store and bought a beer for Bill. Together they poured it down him! Bill could have died without some alcohol. Ask any doctor. The students then checked him into a clinic to dry him out. But they didn't stop there. They loved him into Christ. Unusual and creative evangelistic approach! Right? Bill is now saved, an active Christian. The students coined a slogan to summarize that summer mission: "Ashes to ashes and a beer for Bill." Not exactly a religious slogan. Yet like Jesus, they met Bill and Lois where they were. Then they creatively met their felt needs. They sensed that this would have been the wrong time to moralize, "Keep your mind on your urns and off of beer." That may have been good advice, but very bad timing, and definitely not Jesus' style.

The moment the host ran out of wine at the wedding was not the time for moralizing, either. It was a time for Jesus to creatively care and help by beginning with the man's felt need—rather than rebuking him for his failure.

Someone objects, "But doesn't Jesus ever confront people who do bad things?" Yes, but not when He's trying to raise the faith level of a seeker.

Oh, yes! Jesus did confront rebellious and calloused people. In the Temple He confronted a bunch of religious crooks; they dressed like priests but cared nothing about God or man. They dishonored God by ripping people off. Jesus tipped their tables and cracked a whip and said, "Get out of here." That's what those people *needed*. But not every struggler is a rebel.

Creativity means serving people where they feel pain. Creativity means being sensitive to surface hurts and wounds even though you know the real problem may be deeper. Creativity means helping people as they let you help, not forcing them to take medicine they don't think necessary.

At that moment in old Cana, the people running that wedding were in a state of panic. More good wine was their felt need, and they couldn't see anything else. So Jesus began there.

In an ordinary city, at an ordinary wedding, He met an ordinary human need, but in an extraordinarily creative way. This was "the first of his miraculous signs" that thus "revealed his glory" (John 2:11). God's glory is not that He is a miracle-winemaker, not even that He is a miracle-worker. "Well, I guess I'd better believe in this guy. Look what He can do." But this sign pointed to the glory of Jesus' creative compassion and His disciples *put their faith in Him.* They believed.

In the gospel of John, believing is a *verb*. It's something that you *do*, not something you *hang on to*. In this case Jesus met the felt need of the host in a creatively unique way. He met the man where he was, without passing judgment on the validity of the need, nor on the man for putting himself in this predicament. The disciples "believed." Their "faith action" was that they could go and treat people like Jesus did, helpfully meeting them where they were. All of the power of God went to a wedding and helped—not rebuked—a host off the hook. And that moved the faith of these disciples to a deeper level of understanding. They saw Glory! Through the gospel of John, the disciples kept refining and clarifying their belief in Jesus as they assimilated His people-skills into their lives, so that eventually the glory of God would shine through His followers' faith.

If I am to connect with the felt needs of another, I will need to be vulnerable about my own needs. You will, too. When an insight from Scripture helps you with a certain struggle, just dog-ear that page—either mentally or physically. Later, when you sense a similar struggle in a friend, you can say, "Yeah, sometimes I feel like that, too. But something I read in the Bible helps me." For example, one day when I was feeling like a chunk of dirt, I stumbled across Psalm 103:14, "He knows how we are formed, / he remembers that we are dust." Maybe that doesn't grab you right now, but on that day, it directly connected with my need. I needed so badly to hear God say, "I know how you feel."

Each person feels his or her own unique needs. There are as many felt needs as there are people. But although all people need God, we cannot assume they *feel* that need.

Nor can we assume, as do many believers, that the universal felt need is for forgiveness—that all people feel guilt and long for relief. Thousands of people who are deeply involved in sin feel no guilt at all; at least, they do not identify their feelings as "guilty" ones. They may feel frustrated because they can't manage relationships, or they feel depressed, or stressed, or powerless over chemicals or negative feelings, but they don't associate these feelings with guilt.

Martha caught me at break-time during a seminar. She had just heard me say, "Just as the red light on the dashboard warns us to add oil before we ruin our engine, so a guilty conscience is the red light that keeps us from spiritual disaster. Christians cannot persist in hidden sin without being miserable, and that's good news."

Martha disagreed. She taught Sunday school in her church, had been married to a minister, then two years ago became a thirty-three-year-old widow. Martha confessed that she had become sexually involved with a married man in her church, the husband of a close friend. She had always believed that her conscience would kill her if she ever did anything so far outside of her values, that guilt would eat her alive.

But she said, "In all honesty, I am enjoying this liaison, and I feel absolutely no guilt at all. I must really be sold to Satan!" Martha added that she was terrified precisely because her conscience was *not* bothering her. However, her hands trembled noticeably. She said it was the Valium. "Why the Valium?" "Nerves," she explained. Insomnia. Headaches. Piling on pounds. Chronically upset stomach. Martha felt all these, but Martha felt *no guilt!* She was unhealthy and miserable, but she had never identified any of her feelings as guilt. She took Valium to address the felt needs, the symptoms. But she ignored the real source of her pain.

Since a lot of people do not understand the root and spiritual cause of their misery, Jesus begins with *felt* needs and moves gently toward *real* needs. He begins with our humanity. Of course, He doesn't stop there. His ultimate aim is our spiritual need. With each encounter, Jesus steps into a brand-new drama. To some He gives grace. Others, healing. Still others, a roaring lecture. As we track Jesus through John, we will learn that whether a distraught wedding host or a curious rabbi like Nicodemus, each person is different and deserves to be treated creatively in his or her own zip-coded way. Read on.

Focus:

1. What is the difference between a felt need and a real need?
2. How do we accept people by meeting felt needs without implying approval of sin?
3. Which is most important: the direction people are headed? The speed at which they are travelling? The distance they have come?
4. Recall an instance where you found someone deeply socially embarrassed. How did you react? What would Jesus have done? What would you change now?
5. Have you ever hurried past someone who needed you? Why do you think that happened? How would Jesus have managed that situation?
6. How can you watch for a potential "wedding host" in your life today and "make some wine"?

What's a nice rabbi like me doing looking for
the Galilean at this time of night? My colleagues
back at the Sanhedrin will never understand. They'll
think I'm sneaking around in the dark trying to hide
something. And part of me says they are right.
What does this hick-town carpenter know anyway?
He's no scholar. I'm the one who is supposed to
have the answers!

But God knows my answers aren't working for
me. Haven't been for a long time. Don't even fit my
questions. Maybe He'll have better answers. The
crowds swear by Him. Say they've lost confidence
in the old ways. That I can understand. I keep the
traditions better than most. Even the experts think
so—they appointed me to the Sanhedrin. But no
one has actually gotten much help from my "spiritual counsel."

I guess that's the real reason I'm on my way to
the carpenter. If your religion isn't working for you,
you can't go on recommending it to others. Mine
isn't and I can't. But if that is the case, why am I
afraid someone will see me talking to the carpenter? What have I really got to lose? My reputation,
for starters. Maybe even my livelihood. What does a
man do for a living after he has been laughed out
of the Sanhedrin?

But I'd gladly throw my whole career to the winds for the peace I see in the faces of the carpenter's friends. Well, here I am. If He's got half the power they say He has, I'd best slip up on His good side. Here goes!

"Rabbi, everybody knows You're a teacher from God. No ordinary human being could pull off such wonders . . . all by Himself. . . ."

4

Insiders and Outsiders

Our friend Jim raises hogs. One morning he dropped by the local feed store for a few bags of hog "groceries." Jim slipped the clerk his order, then stepped aside to cool his heels while the bags were loaded onto his truck. Behind the counter he spotted a large wooden sign bearing a painted message for all customers.

Checks are only accepted with:

1. Credit card
2. Local bank account
3. Driver's License
4. Telephone

As Jim waited, another customer stumbled through the

About Talking to Who Is Listening

door. By his uneven swagger and whiskey smell, it was easy to tell that the man had begun to celebrate too early in the day. The drunk staggered up to the counter, blinked a time or two, and slowly read the sign.

Then he turned to Jim with furrowed brow and slurred speech and complained, "They ask too much! A credit card makes sense. Local bank accounts, that's understandable. And someone may even have three driver's licenses, but who do you know that has four telephones?"

Point? Just because a message has been delivered doesn't necessarily mean that it has been understood. A word expressed isn't always an idea communicated. It's not only at Jim's feed store that the clearest sounding messages reach their destination foggy and misunderstood.

In fact, perhaps one of the greatest means of serving others is creative and careful communication. Simply throwing words into the air and assuming you will be understood is neither sensitive nor smart. And it is especially unfair for "church people" to assume the average person on the street can understand our shopworn religious jargon. Many good and intelligent people would love to know our Master if only we would skip the stained glass lingo and introduce Jesus in language that makes sense to them.

Where the Buck Stops

Those involved in Christian communication (which includes all Christians!) must admit where the buck stops. *The responsibility of clear communication lies not so much with the listener as with the speaker.* Of course, the listener has some responsibility. But if we send fuzzy messages, even the most perceptive of people may not clearly decode our signals. And, as the apostle Paul said, "If the trumpet does not sound a clear call, who will get ready for battle?" (1 Cor. 14:8)

Jesus went to incredible lengths to get His point across. He drew inexhaustibly on stories, parables, case studies, and current events. And He didn't tell the same story to every person or even every audience, nor did He spout a repertoire of rehearsed speeches. When Jesus walked in our world, He wasn't just a spiritual presence. He wore clothes just like we do. His feet got dirty and hot and tired like ours do. He hungered. He didn't like flies walking on His food. He strolled our streets through the thick of the people scurrying about daily business.

Wherever Jesus went, He was surrounded by people. He couldn't make it to the market without touching the sick people and well people, rich and poor, young and old, people from all walks of life. Jesus was always in the midst of people. Yet each was precious, and a careful reading of the gospels impresses us with Jesus' creativity in tailoring His communication style not merely to each *audience*, but even to each *individual* He encountered.

Insiders and Outsiders

In John 3 and 4 Jesus encountered two people from very different backgrounds. Their histories contrasted and their felt needs were exactly opposite— one, a religious and cultural insider; the other, a definite outsider. Jesus actually tells the same story two totally different ways to Nicodemus, a Jewish insider, and to a Samaritan outsider.

The communication principles Jesus modeled in these two settings still fit us today. In both conversations, Jesus allowed the lifestyle and location of His message to be determined by the listener, not by His own comfort zone.

First, Jesus was available to Nicodemus. If Jesus had a telephone, His conversation with Nicodemus may have gone something like this:

"Yes, this is He. Tonight? It's 3:00 a.m. Well. Right. Come on over. The porch light is on." Jesus was available, even late at night.

"Hold on a minute, Lynn," you may object. "We don't need to be that accessible to every crank who buzzes us in the middle of the night. Doesn't it bother you that total strangers call you at midnight? Can you always have your life open to interruptions?" Of course, we need boundaries. We are people. Interruptions must have bothered Jesus, too, because He was a "people." But for Him, the balancing question was never "Does this disturb My comfort?" Rather He was concerned with the way His response affected the persons involved.

For example, if I answer every call in the night, eventually I will damage my family. When the call comes, I must clarify my priorities. "At this moment, which is job one: this person calling or the present needs of my family?"

This can be tricky, however. I can become so protective of my family that I shield them from the reality of human need and send my kids the nonverbal message, "Don't worry about the rest of the world. We've got ourselves; our neighbor down the road is not our problem." Balance is the key.

A second person to consider when that midnight phone rings is the person on the other end of the line. Will my response help or hurt? Will it give him or her dignity? It may. Or it may train that person to be further dependent, demanding, and manipulative.

Some think Nicodemus sneaked over to Jesus in the night because he didn't have the guts to go in the daytime, too proud to admit publicly that he might get help from that Galilean carpenter. Well, maybe, but I wonder if Nicodemus may have come at night simply because he was a member of the supreme court (the Sanhedrin), one of the busiest men in all of Israel, and just didn't have time to come in the middle of the day. Point is, he came to Jesus because he felt some kind of need. He was religious. Active. Involved. He tried to keep and teach the Law. But apparently something wasn't working for him. He wanted to know God better. Yet he was so much a part of the system that he didn't know *how* to travel outside his ruts.

A salesman showed up at my door one day saying, "I've flown all the way from New York City to see you because you're one of the leaders of this community, and if I place an encyclopedia in your house, everybody in town will want one." Nicodemus seemed to use a similar approach.

"You gotta be a healer from God. We're all impressed that Your stuff is super-human."

Jesus could have interrupted, "Hey, man. Manipulators I don't respect. Get honest or get out." But Jesus was *sensitive*. He understood that in Nicodemus's world manipulation was standard procedure. So Jesus ignored the style and listened to the heart: "I've come here looking for something, I guess, for spiritual help." And in so many words, Jesus tells him, "I've got what you're looking for."

Straight Talk

Again Jesus is not only available and sensitive, He's *helpful*. But He is also creative—and this time His creativity is terribly direct: "You've got to be born again." Bam! Just like that! Jesus also fit His message to the level of His listener's understanding. What He said to people was determined not by what He had read that morning or heard last Sabbath at the synagogue, but by the needs of the person in front of Him. He found each person at a different spiritual place. So Jesus treated each one uniquely.

Jesus would never have talked this way to the Samaritan woman. She shared almost no basic presuppositions with Jesus. Her understanding was at a very different level from Nicodemus's. But Nicodemus was an insider who shared some fundamental presuppositions with Jesus. Both believed that religion was a good thing. Both believed that if you are going to have a good life you need to have a good relationship with God. Both believed that the Scriptures were the Word of God. Religion, God, and the Bible. A lot of common ground!

Jesus can say to Nicodemus, the "insider," "You're involved in the religious establishment. You're keeping its rules. Something's still missing, right, Nicodemus? But what you need doesn't come by pedigree, precept, or by institutional position, not even through circumcision. It's your heart, Nicodemus. The only hope for you is to have a change in your heart and your nature; a change as total and radical as if you were actually to be born again, a new birth, a spiritual birth.

"No more trust in bloodline, education, or 'religiosity.' Are you ready to glorify God? That means, Nicodemus, you've got to be born again; go through a shift of identity as radical as the one the rabbis require of Gentiles."

In those days if a Gentile converted to Judaism, he was not only circumcised, but took on a whole new

"Jewish" identity, often even changing his name. In fact, one rabbi said that once this transition took place, the identity would have become so radically new that one could marry the woman who was formerly his own mother. The rabbis called this being "born again." Although Nicodemus dodged the impact of Jesus' statement at first, he understood quite clearly the implications of the radical and shocking confrontation of Jesus. "You got that, Nicodemus?" That's insider talk. That's straight.

Because Jesus respected Nicodemus's sincerity and since they shared so much in common, Jesus could go right to the point. He didn't need to build cultural bridges. He didn't clarify vocabulary. He bypassed surface niceties, crossing the bridges that already existed, and immediately declared, "You've got to be born again."

He offered to help by being direct. This, in essence, is Jesus' blunt message to Nicodemus. "Nicodemus, people who don't love the light I'm bringing hide in the darkness so that light won't show them for who they are. You're different, Nicodemus, but you've got to come clean. Open up your heart. That's what you need to do." Oh, yes, Jesus was helpful to the man. But Jesus' helpfulness was *creative*, tailored to Nicodemus's unique position as an insider.

However, Jesus did not assume that all insiders were as sincere as Nicodemus. Quite the contrary. Some of His sharpest rebukes were aimed at "religious people." Jesus pointed out that some people profess "religion" merely to impress other religious people. "Woe to you, hypocrites," declared Jesus, over and over and over (see Matt. 23). He doesn't talk that way to a struggling seeker, nor to those who although ignorant and weak are genuinely seeking God. He does not so bluntly confront the person who does not share His presuppositions. Even for Jesus that would not only be poor communication, but would dehumanize the target of His teachings. Yet with insiders who knew all the vocabulary and how to work the system, those who abused people in the name of God, Jesus didn't mince words.

By Way of Contrast

Jesus' encounter with Nicodemus stands in stark contrast to His conversation with the Samaritan woman in the very next chapter. The Samaritan woman was not a "religious" person. She was a walking question mark in search of God and confused by religion. She came from the wrong side of the tracks. Nicodemus came from the socially elite. Nicodemus came to Jesus' turf. Jesus went to hers. He found her by a Samaritan well.

With Nicodemus, Jesus presents man's response to God's gift, "Unless a man is born of water and the Spirit, he cannot enter the kingdom of God" (John 3:5). Not so with the Samaritan woman. How can she respond to the gift when she doesn't even know what it is? So, instead of telling her how to receive the gift, He stimulates her to wonder what it might be: "If you knew the gift of God and who it is that asks you for a drink, you would have asked him and he would have given you living water" (John 4:10).

Do you hear the contrasting tones of the two conversations? Nicodemus is a religious person who already accepts God. He operates from definite religious presuppositions and within clear-cut institutionalized structure. The Samaritan woman is confused; she wants God, but hears so many conflicting reports on where to find Him and how to worship Him that she has deep doubts as to whether she can ever be acceptable to God. She doesn't seem to trust organized religion.

To Nicodemus, Jesus gives a *way* to respond. To the woman, He gives a *reason* to respond. To Nicodemus He gives a *plan*. To the woman, He gives *Himself*. Because Jesus and the woman live in two different worlds, Jesus carefully constructs a bridge over which He walks from His world to hers.

With Nicodemus we hear the sharp edge of expectancy: "Are you a teacher of Israel and you do not understand this?" With the woman we hear an invitation of hope: "Whoever drinks the water I give him will never thirst" (John 4:13).

Two people. Two entirely different ways of treating people.

Robot Evangelism

One would think this is a very logical principle. "Of course you don't talk to two people the same way." But somehow this principle seldom finds its way into our churches. Perhaps you, like me, have been guilty of laying the same spiel on every person, treating all people the same way, regardless of their background or interest or needs.

Like me you may have loaded your spiritual pistol with a prepackaged clip of verses and an explosively pointed question or two (such as "If you died right now, would you go to heaven?"). Then we go hunting. From door to door, in and out of shopping malls, up and down the streets, every target gets the same ammo. Same questions. Same verses. And what is the result? More often than not, we wind up offending people in the name of Christ rather than building bridges over which Jesus can walk. Then we discouraged soldiers trudge back to camp wondering who really *is* winning the battle.

Am I saying that we shouldn't memorize verses? No. Does this mean we shouldn't witness? Of course not. But I am saying that people are *persons*. Against Satan, we go to war, armed to the teeth, but for souls, we go fishing! To get from insider to outsider turf, we build bridges of relationship. Each person is valuable. Each deserves to be treated with respect, even with a bit of awe. After all, each person is a unique creation of God, and "God don't make no junk."

A Tale of Two Cities

This principle of uniqueness, which applies first to individual persons, applies also to groups, audiences of people, as well. Contrast the approach of Peter in Acts 2 with that of Paul in Acts 17. Both are urgent messages delivered by God's chosen spokespersons. Both are intended to call people to God. Yet the two radically differing audiences call for contrasting styles of language, pace, and presupposition.

In Acts 2, Peter is talking to a crowd of *insiders*. They are not born again, but they are insiders: Jews. Peter calls them "brothers." He appeals to the Old Testament as authoritative and deals with religious concepts familiar to the thousands in his audience.

Paul, on the other hand, in Acts 17, addresses a crowd of *outsiders*. Athenians. Pagans. Not Jews. They don't know the first thing about the Old Testament and certainly aren't likely to be impressed by biblical authority. In fact, they have no Judeo-Christian presuppositions at all, and even the word "God" conjures up a totally different picture. So where does Paul begin?

Paul stands in the public square surrounded by statues and temples to a whole crowd of gods and goddesses. Then Paul says, "By the looks of all these gods around here, I'd say that you people are pretty religious (not a compliment, just an observation). Would you like to know more about the one you call the 'unknown' God?"

No use quoting the Bible to Athenians. It would mean nothing to them. Rather, Paul quoted the Greek poet Epimenides, from a poem entitled "To the Cretan":

They fashioned a tomb for thee, O holy and high
   one;
The Cretans, always liars, evil beasts, idle bellies;
But thou art not dead, thou livest and abidest
   forever,
For in thee we live and move and have our
   being.[3]

Epimenides did not mean Jehovah God. The poem praises his favorite idol. Insiders and outsiders. So by quoting this poem, Paul spoke the language of the Athenians—outsiders' language.

Peter and Paul learned this relational and communication principle from Jesus. He, too, communicated with different people in different ways.

But how does all this roll down our freeways and ride our elevators? Let's make some applications. If we are to treat people the way Jesus did, what does that mean today?

"That's Greek to Me!"

First, obviously it means that we won't use "insider" vocabulary with "outsiders." Jesus spoke the language of the listener. As a reader of this book, you are likely a "religious insider." Your circle may be largely church people. So, as Scripture says, "Be wise in the way you act toward outsiders; make the most of every opportunity. Let your conversation be always full of grace, seasoned with salt, so that you may know how to answer everyone" (Col. 4:5–6). In other words, talk to people in their own language. Choose your words carefully to connect with a person who doesn't share your frame of reference. Each person is unique and valuable and his or her feelings matter to God. Each deserves to be treated with dignity and sensitivity. Hang around church circles even for a short time and you'll hear religious people speak a language all their own, with insider codes, slang, buzzwords, and terms of affection. An outsider who happens upon one of these holy huddles may get an earful as confusing and obscure to him or her as a freshman in a Princeton physicist's lecture.

He might hear weird sounds like: "propitiation," "expiation," "salvation," "reconciliation"! What a vocabulary! "Pre-millennialism," "Pauline theology," "fundamentalism," "Ebenezer," and "Ebon pinion." And the shop talk doesn't stop there. Try to explain these phrases to your buddies at the bowling alley: "for the remission of sins," "born again," "filled with the Holy Spirit," "washed in the blood," and "Kingdom of God." Some inside the circle might figure out what's going on, but to those outside we might as well speak Greek. (In fact, I've even heard some Greek in church!)

Jesus didn't throw around faded clichés or worn-out words. He didn't dump obscure phrases on His listeners, leaving the translation up to them. No, His mind spun tirelessly, persistently searching for fresh, clear, interesting ways to connect with the people on the far end of His conversations.

George, an "insider," says he was riding in the car with Steve, an "outsider." They passed a billboard that gaudily declared, "Jesus Saves." Sensing a window for witness, George, the "insider," asked Steve what he thought of the billboard.

"Oh, I think it's great!" Steve replied.

"Tell me more," George pursued.

"Well, I think it's great that Jesus [pronounced Hey-zoos] didn't blow His money, but Hispanics tend to be thrifty. I save, too!"

Second, in Jesus' communication style, He kept the pace of the listener in mind. He began at *the level of the listener.* Jesus would never have been direct with an outsider like the Samaritan woman in the blunt way He spoke to Nicodemus, the insider. A traveling businessman told me that his best "witnessing technique" was to sit on an airplane or in a restaurant and simply open his Bible and begin reading. If anyone in the vicinity happens to be spiritually hungry, he or she will think "that man over there reading his Bible must be a Christian. Maybe he can help me." He or she will ease over and ask some religious questions. That man's "technique" may open a spiritual conversation with "an insider," someone with religious presuppositions; but if the person near our Bible reader happens to be an "outsider," when the Bible falls open he or she will likely escape to the smoking section or dive behind a newspaper. My friend's approach is exactly the wrong way to connect with an "outsider."

This past week, I did again what I often do. The person sitting next to me on the aircraft said, "My name is Kim and I'm a nurse. What do you do?" I said, "My name is Lynn, and I'm a writer." Sometimes I'm a writer and sometimes I'm a minister. When I feel up for a visit I may tell the person sitting beside me that I'm a writer, which I am. This opens some wonderful conversations. If I'm tired and don't want to talk to anybody, I may admit that I'm a minister, which is also true. That is almost guaranteed to stop conversation dead in its tracks. When Kim asked what I wrote, I answered, "Oh, books, articles, things like that." Then just as the plane touched down, I handed Kim a copy of my book *Finding the Heart to Go On*. She thanked me, opened the book, and saw that it began in the Bible with the life of King David. And you guessed it: end of conversation!

Changing Times

We can expect more and more "religious" conversations to end that abruptly. Fewer and fewer North Americans are reared in religious settings. Outsiders. So parroting "The Bible says" may mean nothing to them. A large percentage don't believe in the Bible. As George Barna points out,

> By 2000, less than half of our adult population will say that religion is very important in their daily lives. For millions of Americans, religion will simply refer to a series of Sunday morning rituals that a shrinking number of traditionalists play. Less than 40 percent of the population will even associate themselves with a Protestant denomination. Barely one out of three adults will include church attendance on their list of things to do on Sundays.
> The '80s were a decade in which millions of young adults gave the church another chance. But relatively few found much that was of per-

ceived value, and the majority have again turned their backs on the Church, perhaps permanently.[4]

How would Jesus relate to them? How should I? Insiders too easily forget. Ask my friend Larry. We chatted in the parking lot after a men's outreach breakfast. He had prepared for weeks and spent thousands on advertising. The plan called for Christian businessmen to invite a tableful of unchurched guests to a breakfast. I was to speak on "Going Deep in Shallow Times." Hopefully this breakfast would spark interest and some would attend a seminar I was leading in that part of the city.

The turnout had been okay. Interest seemed genuine. But Larry was frustrated. He had sat at a table with two other "insiders" and four "outsiders." The insiders talked among themselves about church politics the entire time and virtually ignored the outsiders. Larry overheard similar conversations at other tables. I've experienced this myself. At businesses or civic gatherings, insiders often come up to me and start "church" conversations.

One time I was standing in a service station surrounded by "outsiders," when this "insider zealot" came thundering through the door, grabbed me by the lapels, and launched into some recent "insider" controversy. I could feel the "outsiders" emotionally distance themselves from me—some permanently.

Even at church, not all visitors are looking for a church home. They may be dragged in by a friend. Jesus would be available to those people, but not pushy, probing, or stuffy. And if He were to engage them in conversation, He would speak their language.

Your Place or Mine?

Jesus' approach was also *determined by the location of the listener.* Jesus met each person on his or her own turf. He didn't require the bride's father at Cana to "Come and visit My church." Nor did He consider a Samaritan water well an inappropriate place to talk Messiahship. He was physically available at their location.

Those of us who are "veteran insiders" may not realize the courage it takes for some "outsiders" to walk into a church. The setting is so foreign to outsider culture! Church people *act* funny—some super solemn, others unnervingly ecstatic. "Insider" people *interact* differently, too; they sit in rows and stare at the back of each other's heads and call perfect strangers "brother" and "sister." They sit in silence and eat cracker fragments and drink little shot glasses of wine. Often their music belongs not to here and now, but to then and there.

Jim Dethmer describes it this way:

When I ministered in Baltimore, a heavily Jewish city, I befriended one of the leading orthodox Rabbis in town. This eighty-six-year-old man and I used to get together to study the Old Testament. To show my love for these Jewish friends, I went to synagogue with them on the high Holy days of Rosh Hashanah.

Let me tell you. That synagogue did not set up their service for me. I drove into a strange part of town. I didn't park in the parking lot, in case I felt a need for a quick escape. I walked up to the building. Nobody said hello to me. It was obvious that I was culturally different. Then it hit me that everyone wore skullcaps. I wondered, "What do I do? What are the rules about what you wear?" I saw a big box of skullcaps and put one on. Most of the men wore prayer shawls. What should I do? Though I didn't know whether it was right or wrong, I decided to put one on.

This is an all-day affair and I couldn't find my friends so I walked in and sat down all by myself. Here's the cantor up here chanting in Hebrew. I had no idea what was going on. They were singing music I couldn't possibly comprehend. They were dressed in ways that made me feel totally out of place. No one interpreted things to me. No one informed me what I ought or ought not to be doing. No one made an overture toward me in any way whatsoever.

It was an incredibly Gentile-hostile environment.[5]

This is akin to what "outsiders" usually feel when they first encounter traditional church services. This is the challenge faced by an "outsider" even if he or she is highly motivated to break into "insider" circles. In fact, in order for an "outsider" to understand the "insider" message in some situations he or she may have to overcome even greater social barriers than do Gentiles joining a Jewish synagogue.

So what do we do? Downplay Christian fellowship, Bible study, and prayer circles? Disband the service? No. Worship services have a distinct and indispensable role. But they are for believers, not intended as secular seminars. (Although sometimes a reality check wouldn't hurt to see if the insiders are still tuned in!) If we want to communicate with groups of "outsiders" we must format services or events especially designed to connect with these people. This would make more sense than bringing them to a traditional church service, designed for the nurture of insiders and the worship of God.

But, of course, Jesus didn't sit in church and expect people to come to Him; He went among the people. He sat in their homes. He spoke on their mountainsides. He walked among their sick. He held their children.

And Paul His apostle picked up on Jesus' style: "I have become all things to all men so that by all possible means I might save some" (1 Cor. 9:22). Paul explained that to the Jews he became a Jew. To those outside the law he became as one outside the law. At whatever cost to his own comfort zones, Paul was willing to meet people where they were.

Christian flexibility. Christian sensitivity. Christian adaptability. Call it what you wish, the point is the same: Say "God" in a language people can understand. "Do church" in a way that makes sense!

Some of our best efforts go to care for ourselves. Our best speakers rarely speak to "outsiders." The best thinkers tend to aim their thought-power at "insiders." Even Christian mass media mostly find "insiders" speaking to one another, rather than speaking to "outsiders." How much of this does it take to snuff out interest and desire from outsiders?

Fresh Winds

However, fresh winds are blowing. Here and there at first, but now more and more, we hear of creative ideas paralleling Jesus' creative communication. One congregation converted a barn into a church building in hopes of presenting a friendlier atmosphere. An "insider" family offers an annual block party in their "outsider" neighborhood so they can make new friends. Some Christian radio is totally geared to the secular mind, avoiding religious jargon and phrases, speaking to "outsiders'" felt needs. Contemporary music and drama find their way into our services. Church calendars and programs and styles shift to fit not insiders but "folks that aren't there yet"!

When we catch Jesus' heart for people, creative energy is released not merely to announce, but to communicate.

Focus:

1. Recall a conversation where you have seen an outsider treated like an insider, or vice versa.
2. Have you ever found yourself on the wrong end of such conversations? Tell about it.
3. Describe the best example you can think of when effective Christian communication connected with an "outsider."
4. How can "insiders" improve their witnessing and worshipping style to more effectively connect with outsiders?
5. How do I get started?
6. What would Jesus do?

I first saw Him sitting on the curb of the well in the heat. How strange. A solitary Jew in mid-Samaria? But I tried to ignore Him and go about my work.

When He spoke to me, I froze for a second. A Jewish man *talking* to a Samaritan woman? Centuries of bitterness loomed between our races. And some Jewish men didn't even speak to their own daughters in public, I've heard.

Is He making a pass?

"How come?" I demanded, and I spit the word "Jew" at Him. His reply was courteous, yet sounded like a riddle.

"If you knew who I am, you would have asked Me and I would have given you water . . . living water."

Well, I knew there was no running water here. Not anymore. Thinking back now, my next question was insane: "Are You greater than Jacob?" (I didn't know I was talking to God!)

My heart stopped when He suddenly switched subjects, "Go get your husband."

Why did He say that? My throat closed, and I could tell by the way He said it that He knew about me.

"I don't have one." (It was a lie but not a lie.)

"You have had five."

Old hurts rushed back into my heart.

My first marriage which began with high hopes ended early in failure and heartbreak when my husband threw me out.

The second was worse.

By the time number three came, I didn't really expect much. I felt like damaged goods, useless, hopeless.

When I spoke again, I felt that this Jew understood what was going on in my heart and that He genuinely cared. He was the first man I ever met who didn't try to hurt me! So I asked Him the question that had smoldered for a lifetime in my soul. I longed to know how to find God. Maybe He would know. "On our mountain or in Jerusalem?"

He said where didn't matter. Said God was inside of us. Scary to someone as messed up as I. Couldn't I just figure out who was "right" and forget the "inside"? Sensing my search, He stopped talking about me and started talking about God.

"God is a Spirit. Your heart is on a hunt for Him, lady. You are on the right track. You will find Him if you will be true and genuine."

Still confused, I said, "Well, I know the Messiah is coming!" You see, Samaritans, like Jews, expected a Messiah. "He'll explain all this to—"

His next words fell like lightning and shifted my whole universe. He looked me in the eye and explained softly, "I who speak to you am He."

I dropped my water pot and left it there beside the well. I guess I'll never really need to go back and get it.

5

The Abandoned Water Jar

Back while Carolyn and I were church planting in British Columbia, some of our financial support came from the Mid-Southern states. We often went south for reporting trips. One Sunday afternoon in Indiana, I described an unusual British Columbia wedding I had recently performed. The "wedding chapel" was an old cabin on the side of a mountain in the sagebrush just beyond the timberline. The bride was twenty-seven years old and the groom was forty-seven. They already had two children, and the bride was seven months pregnant. But they were getting married because as brand-new Christians they had come to believe

Stirring Slumbering Hope

that the Lord wanted them to quit living "common-law." Of the handful of wedding guests, five or six were alcoholics, some were drug addicts, one woman was a prostitute who had often sold herself for a case of beer. Another man was on parole—attempted murder. All except two had recently come to Christ. There were no facades, no proud images to protect. At the end of the ceremony, instead of kissing the groom, the bride shouted, "Where's my rolling pin? I've got a license now!" Tears and hugging filled the room. One of my favorite weddings.

But in Indiana when I described the mountain wedding, one "insider" stood and asked, "Don't you ever lead any good Canadian people to Christ?"

I've often wondered since, if Jesus had attended that mountain wedding, what would He have felt? I wonder, too, how this Indiana man would have felt if he'd been sitting at one corner of the Samaritan well while Jesus sat on the other corner when this Samaritan woman showed up.

If there was ever a lady with a wounded soul, she was one. She didn't hide it. She couldn't hide it. It was too obvious. Her shoulders slumped from both the water jar and the weariness of her pain. Her eyes looked tired from ducking condemning glances fired in her direction. Her heart felt scarred and calloused from the train of husbands who had said "I do" with their mouths only to say "I don't" with their lives. Her pace was difficult and slow as if each step was a trudge through the thick mud of her past. Perhaps half a dozen kids, each looking like a different daddy, tagged along, stair-stepped, behind her.

Maybe Jesus wondered what she was doing there at noon. Most people came in the cool of the morning. Perhaps she came for no other reason than that a hot day demanded an extra draw of water. Or more likely, "decent" people didn't come to the well at noon. They cleared out so they wouldn't have to rub shoulders with the riffraff. Perhaps, for this woman, being shoved to this hour with the "trash" wasn't fun, but at least it would cut down on the daily barrage of cheap comments and rude stares.

"Here she comes. They say she'll sleep with any man."

"Her kids are the worst on the street."

"Did you hear that she has a new lover?"

"The last one left her."

It was worth a walk in the hot sun to avoid words that wounded so deeply.

Touching Their Turf

As surely as Jesus wondered what brought the woman to the well at noon, she probably wondered what Jesus was doing there at all! One glance told her that He was a Jew. And in Samaria! What was this Jew up to?

Jews avoided Samaria at all costs. The shortest line from Galilee to Judea ran through Samaria, but most Jews would walk the long way around, an extra fifty miles on foot, to avoid contact with Samaritans. "Might get contaminated." "Hard to buy kosher foods."

But Jesus and His disciples deliberately walked smack into the middle of Samaria. He even stopped at a public watering hole—at noon—the hour of the riffraff, no less. *Available.* Even to this despised Samaritan woman. That's the way Jesus was. His feet tracked the turf of the people He was trying to touch. How can we connect with people if we step around the inconvenient times and unpleasant places where they live their lives? Jesus' heart for people wouldn't let Him dodge the unwanted or steer clear of the unpopular. For Him, each person was of immense value. So there again in Samaria, Jesus deliberately placed Himself face to face with a person that apparently no one else wanted.

Carl Sandberg tells of frequent stands that Abraham Lincoln took against racial prejudice. One particularly stirring drama unfolded on the night of Lincoln's second inauguration ball. He had just delivered the blazing address in which he made famous the words, "With malice toward none; with charity for all, with firmness in the right, as God gives us to see the right, let us strive on to finish the work that we are in. . . ."

That evening, in a White House reception room, Lincoln stood shaking hands with a long line of well-wishers. Someone informed Lincoln that Frederick Douglass was at the door, but security wouldn't let Douglass in because he was black.

Lincoln broke off from high level protocol and had Douglass shown in at once, personally ushering him into the room. The crowd of guests hushed as the great leader appeared at the door. In a booming voice that filled the silence, Lincoln unashamedly announced, "Here comes my friend Douglass!" And then turning to look at his ally, Lincoln said to him, "I am glad to see you. I saw you in the crowd today, listening to my address. There is no man in the country whose opinion I value more than yours. I want to know what you think of it."[6]

This is Jesus' style! Those who see and respect the rich human qualities in individuals whom others reject are pioneers who blaze a trail through thick jungles of bigotry. The next generation can walk on the path cleared by such giants. What further delays might have impeded race relations in this country without Lincoln's heart and courage?

As I write these words, I remember a long-ago wrong that stings like a frozen lash. During our days in British Columbia, we came into an interesting circle of friends. Among them were Indians from a nearby reservation as well as local civic leaders. The local Indian band occupied the low rungs of the social ladder and bore the brunt of racial prejudice. Ironically, I knew that several friends from both the Siwash reservation and the social register battled alcoholism. One Indian who befriended me we'll call Joe Redfox. Joe was a street problem, notorious for wild bouts of public intoxication.

A friend from the other end of the local social ladder with whom I served a term or two in the leadership of the Kiwanis Club was his honor, the Mayor.

Now, in those young and tender days I was quite self-impressed that I "buddied" with no less than the Lord Mayor. The "stinging lash" strikes when I recall one particular Saturday: I was walking down the town's main drag and spied my friend Joe Redfox coming toward me in the next block. Just as Joe raised his hand to greet me and I was about to raise mine in return, the familiar voice of my friend the Mayor called out my name from across the street. I halted my hand before it reached shoulder height, dropped it quick as a flash, wheeled on my heel, and headed across to shake his Honor's hand. I was glowing in the public attention I was getting from the Mayor. At the same moment, I was pretending I didn't even know Joe, much less return his warm personal greeting. My greed for prestige so overwhelmed me that I totally wrote off the dignity and significance of a very warm human being whom I called "friend." Though hopefully God has begun some renovation on my character since, my face still burns with shame at that memory. Why? I was so far from the heart of Jesus. So dehumanizing to my friend Joe.

Throw-Away Person

Jesus was not only available to this woman; God in flesh was sensitive to her. He read the signs that told the story of her troubled life. I don't know how He picked up on all the distress signals. Maybe He'd already heard gossip, or maybe it was some subtle indescribable something about her that spoke to Him of sadness. Who knows? But He realized that life had sent her little kindness. Perhaps John included this story in his gospel because few persons could feel as unwanted as this woman.

Jesus was sensitive not only to the hopelessness of this woman, but also to the great chasm between them. He, a Jew; she, a Samaritan. What do you suppose went through her mind as she walked past a Jew sitting and watching her? He actually opened His mouth to speak to her, "Could you give me a drink of water?" Startled? Then shocked? Then suspicious?

First of all, He had a hostile person on His hands! She was probably hostile toward men in general, but certainly toward this man, a Jew. Race lines in Belfast, Sarajevo, or Saueto could scarcely be more tautly drawn than those ancient lines between Jews and Samaritans. It all began centuries earlier when the Assyrians carried the northern tribes of Judah into captivity. The Jews betrayed their heritage by inter-marrying with Assyrians, thus diluting their bloodline and creating a "mongrel race" called the Samaritans. Their religion became contaminated, too. By the time the Samaritans returned to their homeland, their views of God were greatly garbled.

By contrast, when the southern Hebrew tribes were carried off into captivity, they stubbornly resisted the Babylonian culture. They returned from Babylon to Jerusalem proud that they had compromised neither convictions nor culture. They would remind the Samaritans of southern superiority at the drop of a skullcap. Even when the Samaritans offered to help rebuild the Jerusalem temple, the southern Jews vehemently rejected their assistance, and more bricks were set into the rising wall of prejudice and resentment between Jews and Samaritans. The Samaritans built their own temple, but in 129 B.C. when a Jewish general destroyed it, the slap to Samaritan dignity stung for centuries. Meanwhile, Jewish bigotry only deepened. So the woman who faced Jesus that day belonged to an *unwanted heritage*.

The woman at the well also belonged to an *unwanted sex*. In the ancient Middle East, men did not reward femininity with special courtesies and chivalry. In fact, they systematically degraded women. Some men wouldn't speak to women in public, not even their own wives or daughters. A few were so fanatical that they would literally close their eyes when passing a woman in the street. These were nicknamed the "bruised and bleeding rabbis" because they often collided with walls and trees. (Men today sometimes run into things when they sight a woman coming down the street, but not usually because the male eyes are closed!)

Our water bucket lady was not only humiliated and hostile. She was also *hopeless*. As if it weren't enough to be from a throwaway culture and a throwaway sex, this Samaritan woman seems *unwanted by her own people*. Having gone through five husbands, she was now shacked up with a "lover." Her history of rootless romances draped over her like a sandwich sign, advertising to all that she was a social leper, not welcome at the morning well with proper people. She was a reject, shoved to the edge of humanity, a target of cruel jokes and lustful men. Doubtless she could see nothing ahead but the empty drudgery of the water buckets and wifely bed of a man who wasn't even her husband. Yet her heart hungered for something better. Way down inside of her, she had not stopped wishing that somewhere, sometime, some way, God would touch His people—would touch her!

This woman by the well wasn't an easy person to help. No one would have blamed Jesus if He had pulled His robe over His face and ignored her. After all, He was tired. The disciples were gone, so who would have known? Besides, some would say, if He taught her anything she probably wouldn't have the brains to grasp it, nor the spiritual framework to retain it. And, even if she did, she had no credibility to influence other people, to share it!

But our Master saw a person who matters to God. Weary as He was, He quickly sensed a wounded soul badly in need of bandages and gently moved her into a nonthreatening conversation. He knew He was talking to an "outsider," and He knew He would need to be unusually creative in her circumstances.

The Death of a Salesman

An interpretation of this encounter floated in "sales pressure evangelism" circles some time back. It went something like this:

Jesus asks for water. The woman becomes curious and is disarmed by Jesus' request. When Jesus sees that He has her interest, He manipulates the "water bit" around to "living water." The woman grows more curious. Finally, curiosity makes her vulnerable, and

Jesus zaps her with a trick question about her husband. She ducks her eyes and tries to dodge the question with a half-true answer, "I have no husband."

Then Jesus springs His trap, catches her in her dishonesty, and says, "You are right. You have had five husbands and the one you're living with now isn't really your husband," as if to say, "Aha! Gotcha! You are not only a multiple-affair adulteress, you are also a liar!" At this point, realizing she has been trapped, the woman tries to wiggle out by changing the subject. She poses a theoretical religious question about which temple is the true temple. But it's too late. Jesus nails her!

Now I ask you, does this sound like something Jesus would do? Upon closer examination, this account doesn't imply emotional brutality at all! Skip down to the result of Jesus' conversation. We find this stirring response: "Leaving her water jar, the woman went back to the town and said to the people, 'Come, see a man who told me everything I ever did. Could this be the Christ?'" (John 4:28–29).

Does this sound like a woman who has just been caught lying about her sordid past? Just been snared in the trap of her own embarrassing failures? Why would someone who had just been humiliated by a total stranger run to praise that stranger to her family and neighbors?

And, be honest now, if the town tramp ran up to you and said, "Guess what? I just met a guy at the well who told me every bad secret I was hiding. Come on out, and meet Him so He can *do the same for you.*" Do you think you and the whole town would rush on out to the well? Not likely! Right? But John says the whole town went out to see Him.

What happened then? The key that unlocks this story is found beside the well. The abandoned water jar. And somehow I don't think she ever retrieved the thing. She had no more need to water the last dry sticks of a dead-end relationship. The abandoned water jar speaks eloquently. It says Jesus stirred a slumbering hope to its feet. It declares that this wounded woman found a joy so deep that she forgot to do what she came to do and took off to tell everyone the news, "The Messiah is here!" Instead of dragging heavy jars of tepid water to the house of a demanding human sponge, she piped in living water to all the hearts of a grateful thirsty village.

What had she learned? What did Jesus tell her? Let's return to the first of the story.

Again, Jesus was not only available, He was sensitive. Remember? God came into our world, became flesh, so we could see what God is like. God was sensitive to this woman.

Finding Those Places in the Heart

I find it hard to believe that Jesus crossed His fingers behind His back while asking this woman for a cup of water! It's even more difficult to imagine Christ viewing her as a "spiritual trophy" and the water as bait. No, He saw a person precious to God, a stooped and beaten woman with an authentic heart; and He offered her a first fragment of *acceptance*. By asking for a cup of water, Jesus was saying, "I don't feel the way others do. Your race, your religion, your gender, your past; these don't matter to Me. You are a *person*. You mean something to Me. In fact, *I* need *your* help! 'Could *you* give Me a drink of water?'"

Jesus explains that there is a well of special water—the kind that can quench all thirst. See the wistful look in her eye as she pictures a life with no painful encounters at the well. "Sir, give me this water so that I won't get thirsty and have to keep coming here to draw water" (John 4:15). Can you hear her heart? This man not only accepts her but seems to respect her as she is. What is more, He offers her a way out of her past, a route that does not lead only to some other burdens and some other bed. "Can this man set me free? Dare I believe He could, somehow, actually give me a new start?"

But if this is what she imagined, her daydream of escaping a ball and chain of matrimonial failures is shattered as Jesus actually said, "Go, call your husband and come here." Why? What is Jesus doing? Is He trying to embarrass her into repentance? *Hardly!*

Jesus aches with the emptiness that has stalked the days of this woman's life. When she says, "I don't have a husband," she's not pretending things are different than they are. On the contrary, in essence, she's saying, "He realizes that He has a humiliated person on His hands, someone whom life has not treated well. He also realizes that He has a person that has no hope at all."

"I don't even have a husband. I don't have *anything*." Jesus' response, rather than being a rebuke, implies, "You've had five heartbreaking experiences that have devastated you. Five of them! And now you don't even have a husband. No security. No real relationship. No love and joy and a home you can count on!"

And when the woman asked about the temple, she was not dodging Jesus' point; she was plunging right into the middle of it. She was saying, "That's right.

My life is empty. I need God. Could You tell me where to find Him?"

Jesus cut straight to the source of her pain. Authentic healing only comes when the *true* sickness is treated. Jesus teaches us here the importance of cutting deeper than the superficial and lancing the real source. He is empathizing with the hopelessness that plagued the days of this woman's life. He is extending His hand to her, offering to enter this dark chamber of her world.

Jesus, do I see Your thumb brush a tear from the corner of Your eye? "It must hurt, even after the pain of five desertions, that the man you now live with won't even give you his name."

Jesus and this woman are not standing toe to toe in some type of word game. No, they stand heart to heart; Jesus the master surgeon and she, the grateful patient. What Jesus sees here is not one more wicked whore (as we are prone to assume, but what Scripture does not say), but He sees a brokenhearted woman who is still hungry for God. He sees a person who matters deeply to Him and to His Father.

Terrible Tags

Yes! Before you tag someone "divorcée," you might pause and consider the sting that word carries. When someone loses a mate to death, he or she grieves and we pull alongside him or her and grieve, too. His or her heart is broken, and something is gone that can never be replaced. However, there is usually dignity in the grief.

But when a mate is lost through divorce, the same pain occurs. An unfillable void is created. And there is no dignity in the loss and no real closure. So few flow to the side of divorced people to help them grieve.

Few stand with them in the loss and loneliness. In fact, the opposite usually occurs. Some often look down on the "divorced" through the scopes of judgmental rifles and fire subtle, piercing bullets of accusation. Someone who already feels like a failure in relationships is leveled to the ground by shots of intolerance and lack of forgiveness. This grief has no dignity. Besides, the "corpse" is still walking around.

Let's multiply that cycle by five and see if we can fathom the gaping hole in the center of this woman. It could very well be that she was not a bad woman at all. To me, she could look more like the victim of five or six bad men. Maybe she was plain. Maybe she came from a poor neighborhood. Maybe she couldn't carry on a conversation. Maybe she was missing her two front teeth. We don't know why she was so rejected. Layer by layer, the viciousness of these men had stripped her down until there was little left of the refined things in her nature. But these vicious men had not stripped away her hunger for God, her hope in a coming Messiah!

Can You Tell Me Where to Find God?

What have you felt as you read these words? You may have connected with this woman. Possibly you, too, have long searched for God. Perhaps you, too, have found no answers for those questions that steal your sleep. Maybe, like her, you have heard the endless wrangling and futile arguing among the religious about religion and have walked away from a few visits to church more empty than you came. If so, then read carefully the response of Jesus. It will be of special interest to you.

Jesus got excited! He still does today when He finds pure hunger for God in a broken human heart. He forgot His weariness. He forgot His hunger. He forgot the heat. He lifted the jar off the shoulder of the woman and motioned for her to sit down. And He began revealing truths to her that up to this point He had revealed to no one! That's right—she is the first person to whom Jesus revealed Himself as Messiah!

Let's paraphrase His response. "There is a day coming when the place of worship won't make any difference. You Samaritans worship what you do not know. You've been taught that going to the right mountain and performing the right ritual is how you find God. Ain't so. That is ritual. It isn't relationship."

One can imagine Jesus' finger punching the air as He continued unveiling the truth. "True. Salvation is from the Jews. But the day is coming. . . ." He paused and looked intently in the woman's eyes and disclosed that *the day has come* when the "where" and "when" of worship will not matter. What now matters is genuineness and the spirit of the worshiper. What matters most to God is what is going on in your heart.

He saw her dark days. Felt her hunger. "You are on the right track, lady. You're on the right track! Your heart is hungry for God!"

Now, if you think eavesdropping on this dialogue has been fun up until this point, listen to the woman's next few words: "I know that Messiah (called Christ) is coming. When he comes, he will explain everything to us" (John 4:25).

Look at that! Doesn't that give you a clue to the woman's heart? Here is a Samaritan woman talking about the Messiah! She reveals the hope that has kept her warm on all those cold nights. "In the back of my heart, for all these years, I've been dreaming of the day when God Himself would come so that we could know Him."

High Drama

Oh, can you imagine? Don't miss the drama. It takes my breath away. Don't miss the pure joy and the mist of Jesus' eye as He moves yet a bit closer and says softly, "The one you've been waiting for? He is here. It's Me."

Don't miss it.

That is why she trashed her water jar. That is why she nearly ran over the band of disciples coming up the trail. That is why she stopped the first person she saw in the village and said, "Come and see a man who knows every dream I've dreamt and every tear I've wept! He felt my pain when I was taken to the door that first time and my husband called the neighbors around and said three times [as was the custom], 'I divorce you.' He heard me crying on my lonely bed all night. He knew why I settled finally for a 'live-in.' He also knew those long nights my heart cried out for God. I've hoped for Him and longed for Him. Could it be that He is the Messiah? It seems almost too good to be true. But I think I just *gave a cup of water to God*. Now this man has come, and the cords that were broken will vibrate once more. I have hope."

Oh, we need to be like Jesus. The living water is not found in a holy house in Jerusalem or a holy hill in Samaria; and for this woman, not even in a happy home. But the holy place, the temple where God comes to live, is a hungry heart! That's what it is. And that is the vessel in which to carry home the living water.

Love always sees the best; it always looks for the best. Jesus was looking for what was in this woman's heart. A little child of a Texas friend wanted to get a birthday present for his mother. He'd heard one of the older sisters say that his mother wanted a new slip. Now, he didn't know what a slip was. But he went shopping. When he stood in the ladies' department and was shown a slip, although he was mortified with embarrassment, he was still determined to buy one for his mother. The clerk asked, "What size does she wear?"

"Well, I don't know."

"What is she like?"

"Oh, my mother is just perfect."

So the clerk packaged up a size 34 and sent it home. Next week his mother brought the 34 back and changed it for a size 52! Love sees the best. And Jesus saw the best in this Samaritan lady, a *tender* heart nearly buried forever at the core of the woman's *tough* life.

Drop Your Sandwich and Open Your Eyes

Jesus' disciples came back from their shopping trip and found Him standing by the well with a big grin on His face as He stared at the disappearing figure of a woman who was hot-footing it toward town. The disciples didn't know what happened. Jesus volunteered no explanation, and they lacked the courage to ask. One of them handed Him a sandwich, and He turned it down. He was too excited to eat.

"Open your eyes," He told them. They looked up as the excited woman disappeared around the curve of the trail. "Look at the fields! They are ripe for harvest" (John 4:35). A few minutes later a crowd of Samaritans appeared around the same curve, with the same woman leading the pack. Smiling. Laughing as if someone had just told her a joke! Last time she came down that trail she was alone, carrying a heavy water pot and a heavier history of pain. This time, however, she comes with friends. This time she comes unburdened and jubilant. "There He is!" she cries. They have come to invite this newly found Messiah and His friends to their city.

Jesus was creative. Talk about creative! Imagine the captivating scene. A handful of young Jews walking into town side by side with a group of curious Samaritans. On any other day if these two factions were found together a fight would surely be brewing. But this time they are drawn together by a common hunch, a common hope, that this unassuming carpenter might . . . just might . . . be the One they've been looking for.

So the crowd headed back to town, following an odd couple: a Jewish man and a Samaritan woman; a rabbi and riffraff; incarnate God and a single mother; a long-sought Messiah and a long-rejected misfit! But as one follows this Man/God on His brief earthly journey, we grow accustomed to His entourage; we frequently find Him flanked by assorted cast-offs. Tax-collectors, harlots, crooks, thieves—they seemed to flow to Him. Somehow they perceived that although He knew their darkest secrets, He was willing to forgive them. He felt their sharpest pain, too, and their deepest hunger, their longing for God. Somehow they detected that He could bring cleansing to their lives stained with forbidden fruit and newness into their stale worlds.

Calvin Miller in *The Singer* writes:

"Listen while I sing for you
a song of love."
He began the melody so vital
to the dying men around him.

She listened and knew for the
first time she was hearing all of

love there ever was. Her eyes swam
when he was finished. She sobbed and sobbed
    in shame. "Forgive me,
Father Spirit, for I am sinful
and undone . . . for singing weary
years of all the wrong words. . . ."

The Singer touched her shoulder
and told her of the joy that lay
ahead if she could learn the
music he had sung.

He left her in the street and
walked away, and as he left, he
heard her singing his new song. [7]

This is the joy Jesus offered to the woman at the
well and to us.

The Real Miracle

Much ado is made over the way Jesus healed
physical illnesses. And we also cover our mouths in
awe at the way He mastered the storm or sent a dozen
shrieking demons into the deep. Appropriate re-
sponses. But once we watch Him treat the gaping
wounds of this nameless woman . . . once we see the
balm that He could so carefully place upon lacerated
souls . . . that's when we are left most amazed. Here
is where the Great Physician did His greatest healing.
Here is where He performed His most majestic miracles and stilled His greatest storms: when He is
stitching together the ragged lives of unwanted people.
    Want proof? Look back at the well. The water jar is
still abandoned. Want more proof? A whole town

came out to meet the One who cared enough to notice "everything they had ever done"—and to love them in spite of it. In fact, to love them out of it!

Focus:

1. How does Jesus cross the great chasm between Himself and the woman at the well?
2. What helps you see beyond someone's pain to the source of sickness? How does true healing come?
3. What principles of Jesus can you use to bring about healing in some strained relationships?
4. Who is your Samaritan woman and where is your well?

*E*ven from five feet above the pavement, the place smells bad enough. Garbage. Animal droppings. Stinking feet. Vomit. Used bandages. From my angle, it's far worse. My nose rarely gets more than belt-high. But, I'm used to this kind of life after thirty-eight years. Sure, I sit on a hard pallet and beg every day, enduring abuse from passers-by. But I'm secure. I've never gone to bed hungry. An endless stream of do-gooders keeps dropping coins in my cup.

But I whine anyway. So lonely. Pallet too far from the foot traffic. Smell gets to me. Mat gives me bed-sores. Life isn't fair. No one ever gives me a break, not even a helping hand. Once every day the healing angel stirs the pool. First cripple in gets healed. But never me. Some other cripple always gets there first. And the able-bodied don't give a tinker's hoot. So, if you could just drop an extra coin in my cup, old friend, God will be sure to smile on you. Thanks. Obviously you're one of the few who does care about people like me.

What's that? The carpenter has come here? Yeah, they say He just lives for helpless people like me. He'll look me in the eye when I talk. He won't be stingy with His company, nor with His coins. Look. He's glancing my direction.

Here He comes. Why is He looking at me like that? Do I want what? What kind of question is that? Am I really sure I want to be . . . ?

6

Escaping the Victim Mentality

In the movie *Born on The Fourth of July* Tom Cruise plays a Vietnam war veteran who is wounded, paralyzed from the waist down, and sent home. The young man who had been the picture of health, independence, and competitiveness merely sits around feeling sorry for himself and drinking. His self-pity drifts to rage. Then his rage shifts from bad to worse, until he alienates himself from his old sweetheart, his friends, and even from his own parents.

He hits the lowest point in his miserable life when he runs from relationships and reality and dives into a drunken tour of Mexican bor-

From Patronizing to Personizing

dellos. But even a second-string prostitute spurns and ridicules him for his victim mentality. Once he has hit this all-time low he finally begins to get hold of himself. The movie has a happy ending, when Cruise forgets his self-pity and takes charge of his life. But few people who have fallen into the "victim mentality" ever leave their pity party and get on with life. In fact, all too many of us learn how to get mileage out of our misery, duck responsibility with our loser's limp, and milk our misfortune for all it's worth.

Sue, for example, enjoyed her pity party. When Sue was the star of her high school track team, she sprained her ankle in practice. The doctor put her on crutches. The week prior to her injury, Sue had lost badly for the first time ever in the one hundred meter race to Bitsy, a long-time rival. Sue stayed on crutches for a whole week after the doctor said her ankle was ready for running. That kept her out of the next track meet in which she was scheduled to run a rematch against Bitsy.

In the meantime, Sue made a discovery: Without winning, or even competing, she was showered with more attention, especially from the boys, than she ever had received from athletic victories—*until* all the boys began to catch on and grow weary of her pity party. Then Sue found herself surrounded only by the losers and nerds who were attempting to raise their own social stock by "being tight" with the once-popular school celebrity.

Hooked

Doubtless, a lot of us are susceptible to the alluring and addicting drug of self-pity. We may get turned on to this "angel dust" of the spirit, first during a period of adversity, through the good intentions of kind people. And the kindness feels so good, we keep coming back to the well. With time, we become "pity junkies." Our "helpers" become codependents. We thrive on the compassion and attention of others. We yearn for someone to notice our plight or ask about our pain. At best our life is reduced to one objective: hunting for comfort and delegating our recovery to others; at worst, copping out of responsibility and blaming someone else for our problems.

Our conversations focus on ourselves; why we are sick, how much it hurts, how harsh the world is to us, why we are losers, and other assorted rationalizations for failure. We blame anyone, everyone, anything but ourselves. We become masters at reciting our woes. We hold out our tin cup to all who pass, begging for a listening ear.

"My boss doesn't respect me." "My children don't appreciate me." "Society expects too much of me." Or, as my mother used to chide, "Nobody loves me, everybody hates me; I'm going to the garden to eat worms." Finally we wind up miserable. We can't go on without our "attention fix," yet we don't like ourselves for needing it. We resent the very people we depend on to give it to us. Bottom line is—we get angry at ourselves, at others, at circumstances—till the quiet, bitter rage poisons every motive and every relationship. We feel unable to function and convince ourselves that we cannot. Finally, dreams die, and self-respect and normal feelings of compassion and hope wither.

Do you know some people addicted to self-pity? No doubt you do. And no doubt you know they are not easily helped. For one thing, it's difficult, if not impossible, to help someone who wants to stay helpless. For another, it's easy to get nauseated on his or her unending recital of personal mishaps and tragedies.

And it *is* risky! You may wind up being the target of blame, or overloaded with "leaners," or even sucked into a codependent relationship.

Would you like some insight on how to help those imprisoned by self-pity? To help this junkie kick it cold turkey? What do you suppose Jesus would have to say to people who live that way? Read again the story of His healing the paralytic in John chapter 5. You might recognize the four principles that Jesus teaches here.

- Be where people are.
- Be sensitive to people.
- Be helpful to all people.
- Be creative—each person is unique and valuable.

Out Where the People Are

The man at the pool of Bethesda is a classic case of what we are talking about. Thirty-eight years as an invalid. Plenty of time to become thoroughly convinced that he would never get better and that the world was enemy number one. Plenty of time to develop an addiction to the life of moaning, pity hunting, and blaming.

What a grim scene Jesus found at the pool. John said "a great number of disabled people used to lie" there (John 5:3). Bodies everywhere, groans, complaints, stench, begging—a scrap heap of broken-down people.

Some years back, I accompanied a friend as he traveled for treatment to M.D. Anderson Cancer Center in Houston, Texas. Most of my adult life, I have been no stranger to hospital visits. But I was not at all prepared for what I saw at this massive complex known across the nation for excellence. Instead of a handful of patients with minor ailments conversing in a small waiting room, I saw large halls filled with crowds of sufferers from across the country. All were strangers to each other. Most were desperately ill and living with the terror of a life-threatening disease. As far as the eye could see: little children, chemotherapy patients with pale eyes looking blankly from hairless heads, elderly people who couldn't hold their heads erect, middle-aged skeletons pushing IV machinery ahead of their shuffle, loved ones with dark circles under terrified, tear-filled eyes. The clinical silence was disturbed only by the occasional groan or the racking sound of dry heaves.

As I sat waiting with my friend, I found myself thinking, surely this is the modern, high-tech equivalent of the smelly suffering under the covered colonnades surrounding the pool of Bethesda.

Again, the obvious may elude us: The simple fact that Jesus was at this pool is worth noting. He was where the hurting people were—available—even to a collection of "leaners." When we know that someone is a "pity-junkie," what do we normally do? If you know that a visit with so-and-so will end up with your being dumped on, do you want to go? Usually not. Life is already loaded with responsibilities, entanglements, negativism, and bad news. Who wants an earful of someone else's aches and pains? Who wants another draining dependent? Who wants to go where everyone feels sorry for herself or himself?

Jesus does.

That is the way He is. The nature of Jesus is to go to those who hurt. Were He physically here today, He would be with the people in convalescent homes, hospitals, and mental asylums. If Jesus worked at your job, He would seek out the hurting people. But not just among the physically sick. He headed into all kinds of human misery. He wouldn't sidestep the inner city, with the winos, panhandlers, bag ladies, and cripples. And if my faith never leads me to these places and people, then maybe I should reexamine my faith.

As George MacLeod said,

I'm recovering the claim that Jesus was not crucified in a cathedral between two candles, but on a cross between two thieves; on the town garbage-heap; at a crossroad so cosmopolitan that they had to write His title in Hebrew and in Latin and in Greek . . . at the kind of place where cynics talk smut, and thieves curse and soldiers gamble.[8]

Walking in Another Person's Mind

Not only was Jesus available to people in physical pain, but He seemed specifically sensitive beyond what ailed this crippled man's body to what ailed his soul. Jesus was not only willing to go to the mat with this man—but looked beyond the obvious to ask what brought the man to the mat! "Jesus saw him lying there and learned that he had been in this condition for a long time" (John 5:6). "He learned. . . ." Apparently Jesus did a little asking around, gathered some information.

A few mornings back, a man stood not three feet from my car at the traffic light. His hand-lettered cardboard sign read, "I am homeless. My children need food. Willing to work." He eyed a ten-dollar bill lying on my dashboard. So I rolled down the window and without saying a word, shoved the bill into his hand. The light changed and I was gone.

I'm pretty sure I gave the ten to him for my own benefit. I felt better, but only briefly. Then I began wondering whether I had helped the man or dehumanized him. I certainly never acknowledged him as a person. I have no idea what he did with my ten dollars. He may have had no children and plenty of food. May have spent my money on drugs. He knew I didn't care enough to find out.

Later that day, I worked a few hours at an inner-city ministry of our church that distributes food and clothing. Here I interviewed another fellow who greatly resembled the man I'd seen at the intersection. Following a form developed by the director of the center, I asked questions. Address? Social security number? Proof that he had applied for food stamps? I checked out his story. Reviewed his records. I asked about his family, his health.

Then I walked him through our employment resource and invited him to join our life-skills class where he could upgrade his employability. And although I never gave any of my own money and got no emotional buzz, and even though at some points my questions felt discourteously nosey, still I felt much better about my encounter with the second man.

I think it was more like Jesus to do a little asking around. It is usually assumed that the man in John 5 was paralyzed. But the Bible doesn't specifically say that. Could his illness possibly have been psychosomatic? Had he just talked himself into paralysis? We don't know. But as we follow his story, we suspect it.

Are You Sure You Want My Medicine?

We get some clues from the way Jesus dealt with him. Jesus didn't avoid the down and out. But, then, He didn't enable anyone to be codependent, either.

Up front Jesus asked, "Do you want to get well?" What tone of voice flavored Jesus' question?

Does the voice of Jesus here sound like the compassionate shepherd? Trembling, on the verge of tears? I don't think so. Of course Jesus felt compassion, and no doubt there were certainly times when His voice quivered and His tears flowed. But not likely this time.

This time I hear our Master's voice sounding firm, direct, compelling. The Greeks could hear it clearly in the verb tense. He's challenging the man to dump his denial, to get honest, to accept responsibility. He is telling the invalid to face up to himself. Jesus is asking, "Do you *really* want to be healed? After all, you've got a pretty good thing going here. Your tin cup always gathers enough coins to buy your daily beans and bacon. You have eaten three square meals a day for thirty-eight years. Everybody feels sorry for you. You have a lot of people looking out for you.

"If I were actually to heal you, Monday morning you'd have to be down at the unemployment office. At thirty-eight years of age with no job record, you'd have a hard time getting work these days. And when you find employment, you could get fired, or laid off, or criticized, or overworked. Are you really sure that you want to get healed? To face the facts?

"I'm offering you an opportunity to become a person. Will you quit playing games and own up to your addiction?"

In His few crisp words, Jesus probes that man's heart and leaves the man wondering. Why didn't the man react to Jesus with something like, "What kind of question is that? Of course I want to be healed. After thirty-eight years, what would *you* want?" But instead, the man's response is defensive. He complains! He rationalizes!

Inadvertently, in his whining, the man further reveals his own spiritual paralysis. He tells a tale he has likely told ten thousand times, "Well, thirty-eight years and I've never made it to the pool. I'm a cripple, you see. Can't walk. Someone always gets to the pool before me. All these people stand around here, and no one helps *me*. It's their fault I'm not healed!" Meanwhile, we can't help but wonder if Jesus is thinking something like this, "Thirty-eight years? Your body may be crippled but your head isn't. Some days, instead of begging for a shekel, you could have asked for a shove. At the rate of one awkward flop a month, after thirty-eight years you would surely have rolled as far as the pool."

Taking Charge of Life

In 1965, psychiatrist William Glasser wrote a book entitled *Reality Therapy*, which challenged a deterministic psychological theory popular at that time. Glasser may have shifted the whole shape of psychology over the last three decades. He simply insisted that people are responsible for what they do. In the decade before Glasser human foibles of all sorts were usually explained by digging around in the past. How did your parents treat you? How were you potty-trained? Society is to blame for the way you turned out. But Glasser insisted that while all of those factors may be important, they are not determinative—that we do what we *choose* to do, and that we must accept responsibility for our behavior.

One of my first introductions to Glasser was an article in which he described an interview with a young runaway who survived by prostitution (although she had come from an affluent family). When she sat down in Glasser's office, he asked about her difficulty. She said, "I'm emotionally disturbed."

Glasser responded, "Our girls aren't here because they are emotionally disturbed, only because they violated the law. If your only trouble is being emotionally disturbed, I will make it my business to get you out of here because we don't understand anything about complicated psychiatric problems like that."

The girl grinned because she had gotten a lot of mileage out of that diagnosis. This girl had become an expert at ducking responsibility for her own behavior.[9] What would Jesus have said to her?

A troubled college sophomore came by to talk with me. He longed to be a doctor but had little hope of it because his parents had not "done a good job of teaching him how to be responsible." So he didn't know how to study. He was flunking out of school.

He came by again some time later. He'd married, but his wife had left him. He was still angry at his parents. They "hadn't taught him how to manage relationships." But he was also angry at his wife because "she couldn't help him be happy." Besides that, he was angry at the church because the church "didn't help him keep his marriage together."

I saw him again a few months later; he had already remarried. Some time later, he called again. The second wife had left him, and he'd been fired. Not only was he angry at the parents, the wives, the church—now he was angry at his boss because he was out of a job as well. And if I was any kind of "man of God" I'd understand how life had victimized him! What would Jesus have said to him?

Look at the next thing Jesus does with the man at Bethesda. Jesus was *creative* in the way that He reached into that man's life. Three big things can happen to people in such circumstances. First, some people can be *paralyzed*. But the physical paralysis is only the small issue here. The larger issue is that the man was psychologically paralyzed. He was crippled in his soul! Somehow along the way he had convinced himself that he was helpless. A victim!

"*Get up!* Pick up your mat and walk." Jesus spoke in direct, demanding, confrontational language. He challenged the man to take responsibility for himself. He demanded that the man go cold-turkey. He yanked the mirror out of the fellow's hands and forced him to look at the world again. And Jesus was creatively helpful, because whether the man was really physically sick or just emotionally sick, Jesus healed him. He said, "Get up! Pick up. Walk." Jesus' words were aimed at more than the withered legs on the bedroll. He straightened a crippled personality.

This healing is not an easy thing to do. In fact, it would have been much easier for Jesus just to listen to the fellow's woes and whines, pat him on the head, whip up a few miraculous loaves and fishes, or dump some celestial silver in the man's palm, and go back about His business. It is never easy to confront someone with his or her own addictions and illusions. But tough love doesn't always do the easiest thing.

The Big Sin

What is more, Jesus called the victim mentality a *sin* (v. 14). When a person becomes so enveloped in a cocoon of the sin of self-pity that he or she is suffocating, drastic action is required. One doesn't treat cancer with a Band-aid. A flood can't be held back with tissue paper. And some "heart conditions" are so advanced that they call for "open heart surgery."

Want some examples?

Remember Simon the Sorcerer (Acts 8)? He was the sweet-talking magician who wanted to buy the ability to give the gifts of the Holy Spirit. But when he made Peter a business proposition, the apostle showed how he earned the nickname "Rocky."

> Peter answered: "May your money perish with you, because you thought you could buy the gift of God with money! You have no part or share in this ministry, because your heart is not right before God. Repent of this wickedness and pray to the Lord. Perhaps he will forgive you for having such a thought in your heart. For I see that you are full of bitterness and captive to sin."
>
> (Acts 8:20–23)

It wouldn't be too long, however, before Peter would walk the other side of the street. It seems that he compromised a bit on the grace of God because he was intimidated by the law-conscious Jews. When there weren't any Jews in town Peter buddied around with every Gentile in the church. Yet when one of the Jews came visiting, Peter gave the uncircumcised Gentiles a cold shoulder.

Cures That Don't Cure

The hypocrisy came to an abrupt halt when Peter ran into a stick of dynamite called Paul. Paul knew that before things can get better, sometimes they have to get worse. He felt that brothers had a responsibility to bring out the best in each other, even if that was done at the painful expense of cutting off the worst. Paul's description of the scene is brief but sufficient: "I opposed him to his face, because he was in the wrong" (Gal. 2:11).

Now, wait a minute, Paul. Isn't that overdoing it? What about patience and longsuffering? Whatever happened to brotherly love? It is possible to patronize people. Of course there are many times when listening and sympathy are the perfect ways to help someone. In fact, in a world as love-starved as ours, most of us could use a gentle stroke or two. But there are also times when a compassionate ear only feeds a raging addiction. There are ways of "helping" that are not "helpful." There are times when love demands that we abandon the position of a listener and assume the task of confrontation, and there are times when doing what looks compassionate is actually a cruel thing to do. Examples:

- delivering a Thanksgiving turkey or a Christmas fruit basket to a needy family across the tracks without even learning their names, and with no contact the rest of the year.
- shoving money into the palm of a panhandler, rather than accompanying him on a shopping tour of the supermarket, capped off with a visit over a Big Mac, or offering him yard work for pocket money.
- dropping everything again and running to bail out seventeen-year-old Susie when she has let her car run out of gas for the twentieth time this month.
- taking Johnny to Dairy Queen to console him after he lost his starting spot as wide receiver because he skipped practice twice last week, and all the while laying the blame on the coach for being unfair.

We never help a person recover his dignity and initiative by rewarding and reinforcing dependency and irresponsibility. Jesus didn't. We shouldn't.

When Carolyn and I were planting one new church, we had to get up early Sunday mornings, go down and sweep out the rented hall, and set up the chairs for services. Then we'd go and pick up people in our car. If we picked them up, they'd be in church. If we didn't, they didn't bother to come. We were going to make sure that they got to church, and in so doing, we reinforced their dependency by taking responsibility for their behavior. We even learned later that some of these people actually hid under their beds at times to keep from being picked up!

There is a difference between making a person feel like a project and helping him or her to become a person. Some parents repeatedly bail their kids out of speeding tickets and bills and blame their coaches and teachers for everything that goes wrong, and the kids grow up to be emotional cripples. They don't know how to handle anything. Some try to stay in college as long as they can because "Daddy said that as long as I stay in college, he'll pay the bills."

That same principle can operate in marriage, too. Sometimes one person takes responsibility for the happiness of the other person; the other person says, "Okay, you promised to make me happy. It's your fault that I'm not." Eventually both are miserable, and it's the "other person's fault." We can't do for others the things they really need to do for themselves. We cannot "fix" people.

Of course, this principle holds as true with groups as it does in individual relationships. Some kinds of Christian charity, intended as acts of love and assistance, actually wind up damaging people and proliferating hurtful systems. As Roger Greenway and Timothy Monsma write,

> Churches and mission agencies that hand out food and clothing month after month and year after year are not really tackling poverty. Things need to be done that will break the poverty cycle for individuals, families, and neighborhoods, and lift people to a level where they can provide for themselves adequately and with dignity. Long-term relief only creates dependency and dependency is debilitating and dehumanizing. It is tragic that so much of Christian concern for the poor has been expressed in ways that create and maintain dependency relationships. As a consequence, large numbers of poor people have lost confidence in their ability ever to rise above poverty; they have resigned themselves to living off the benevolence of others. . . . There is a better way of conducting development ministry, but it requires a firm commitment to using available resources in the most efficient manner, so that the poor are not merely fed and clothed today, but are empowered to meet their own needs, and the needs of their neighbors, tomorrow.[10]

You're a Big Boy Now

The third piece of advice Jesus gave the man at the pool is found in verse 14, "Stop sinning or something worse may happen to you." This phrase raises two questions: "Sinning? When did the man sin?" and "What 'worse' thing could possibly happen to him than already had?"

After Jesus got the fellow on his feet, the guy had headed down the street carrying his mat, only to be stopped by a "church cop" who interrogated, "Why are you working on the Sabbath?" Rather than accepting responsibility for his own decision and his behavior, the former cripple reverted toward his old victim illusion. "Not my fault, man. It's His." And he fingered Jesus with the blame. So Jesus said, "Don't do that anymore. You are responsible for yourself! Don't slip back into your old victim pattern. You've been *sinning*—sinning against *yourself*."

The man had been sinning ever since he started feeling sorry for himself. Whenever a person sins against himself, he sins against God. God is calling us to something better than that—to make deliberate, volitional choices. That's why Jesus warned, "Don't sin anymore."

The result? In the closing scene of this drama, we see the man interrogated by one more Pharisee, but this time the man carrying his mat also carried his own responsibility: He admitted that Jesus had healed him. In other words, "*I* made a decision to accept Jesus' healing and to follow Him. *I will accept total responsibility for the consequences of that decision.*"

Some penetrating questions we may need to ask ourselves:

- Do I want real healing?
- (or) Do I want to hang on to my story?
- If I've been blaming someone else for my failure and my ungodliness and my self-centeredness, do I want to live with the illusion that I'm a victim or will I accept the painful but responsible reality that I can choose to get out of this trap?

Do-Gooders

Viktor Frankl said, "The last of human freedoms is the freedom to choose one's attitude regardless of the circumstances."[11] Paul said, "For God did not give us a spirit of timidity, but a spirit of power, of love and of self-discipline" (2 Tim. 1:7). When you accept responsibility for your life, God gives you the power to follow through! But He won't take responsibility from or for you.

Being a "fixer" is also addictive. The Messiah complex. The feeling of power and significance surging through us when people "cannot make it" without us. (Especially if they also give you a hundred dollars an hour.) Of course, legitimate counseling and therapy are valuable and helpful, but not the maudlin codependency that goes with some of the "shade tree mechanic" kind of "do-gooding" we easily get drawn into. This raises another set of questions which might clarify what we are up to:

- Am I a "do-gooder" trying to make myself look nice without any regard to how my "helpfulness" is enabling helplessness in others?
- Or do I want to cling to the addictive illusion that I'm really helping?
- Will I learn to painfully, gently confront the realities in myself and the hurt in the eyes of my codependent friend?

The phrase "self-pity" embraces the word "pit" in its bosom. How cryptically symbolic! A pit is the result of self-pity, a pit big enough for one person and no one else. The air is putrid with selfishness, and vision is blocked by the walls of narcissism.

That is why Jesus calls it a sin! "Stop sinning," He said. "Stop or something worse will befall you." Instead of *paralyzing* or *patronizing* people, Jesus *personizes* people. That word is an Anderson original, but don't forget what it means. It means *helping people become persons*. That's what Jesus did. He deftly helps separate the victim's illusion from the reality of personhood.

Jesus' jolting warning is intended for us all. Play with the drug of self-pity, and you will be digging your own pit. And with each spade of dirt that you throw out, you will be farther away from God. Self-pity *is* a sin. It focuses all of our attention inward. It elevates the self instead of the Savior. And those who would follow God are told to deny self, not pamper it.

Getting Clean

Now to Jesus' second warning for this man. When Jesus said, "Something worse may happen to you," He wasn't threatening the man. He was explaining the facts of life. The life that becomes wrapped up in itself makes a pretty small package. There is certainly not enough space for someone as big as God. Those who choose that muddy pit of self-pity are actually doing so at the expense of knowing God. That's a mighty high price for a little attention.

The very name of this addictive drug suggests its cure. *Self*-pity cannot exist if self is dead. We can't feel sorry for ourselves if there is no "self" to feel sorry for.

Are you suffering from the addiction to self-pity? Is your initiative atrophied by your love for self? Do you relish the attention that others give you? Have you been abusing listeners with your whines and woes and been getting by on your loser's limp?

Jesus also said, "Whoever wants to save his life will lose it, but whoever would lose his life for my sake will find it" (Matt. 16:25).

Do yourself a favor. Throw away your needle. Flush your pills. You don't need any more drugs. Get up off your self-made mat and walk. You *can* walk. It doesn't matter if your spouse doesn't always care or if your boss doesn't like you or if your parents spanked you too much. Get up! God is greater than these things.

God has taken the first step. Now you have to take the second step. God is ready to heal you, but He won't help you as long as your medicine cabinet full of self-pity is more important to you than knowing Him.

Focus:

1. What is the victim mentality? Describe a person you know who has it.
2. Tell about a time when you or someone you know didn't really want healing.
3. Is there any story you may be clinging to right now at the expense of reality? If so, what is it?
4. What is the first step you can take to distance yourself from self-pity?

Okay. So some people call me tight-fisted. But it doesn't take me long to reach the bottom line. And His idea was worse than impractical. It was impossible!

Before sunrise we had been mobbed with people. So we jumped in a boat, paddled across the lake, and climbed the hill just to get some peace and quiet. But it didn't work. The mob sniffed us out like bees would honey, and here they came again, swarming up the hill toward us.

These people had tracked Him since dawn. They were pooped. And starved. Apparently food hadn't seemed important when they left home. But by now they had burned energy for hours and had eaten nothing.

To our surprise, the carpenter welcomed them as if all five thousand were expected dinner guests. Then He turned and asked me to find them food. Had He lost His mind? There wasn't a bread crust within a day's travel. Besides, if there had been a supermarket next door, who could afford to shop for that mob? One meal alone would eat up eight months of a fisherman's pay!

What He said made no sense! Yet, something about the way He said it sent a shiver of anticipation up my spine.

Then Andy piped up, "This kid over here wants to share his sardine sandwich. It's not much, but it's a start."

Sure, Andy. Sure. Andy has a good heart. But he can't count. Sometimes he is about as practical as three left feet.

Then the weirdest thing happened. The carpenter seated the crowd on the grass, said grace over the sardine sandwich, and started passing out pieces to the people. Only a kid's trail-snack. But the whole mob binged till they burped and left a dozen baskets full of scraps.

He is the one who did it. The carpenter. Yet, Andy, the kid, and I—each felt that . . . well . . . that somehow . . . we had done it, too!

7

Different Strokes

Bill Hybels cautiously refers
to God as a "variety junkie."
Bill does not mean this irrev-
erently. He means that "God
has a thing about differentness. . . . I look around creation and sometimes lovingly
accuse God of creative over-
kill. Did you know there are
three hundred thousand species of beetles? Now I ask you,
wouldn't fifty thousand of
them have been enough? . . .
Isn't three hundred thousand
sort of piling on?" But God's
creative genius also designed
variety among human beings.
Hybels further comments that
"when each of us understands
his or her unique circuitry
maybe we can celebrate it.
Maybe someday even be able

*When One
Size Won't
Fit All*

to fall to your knees and worship God for wiring you up exactly the way He did!"[12]

God graciously and creatively designed us to both give and need different kinds of strokes. He made no two people exactly alike. Just as our fingerprints are unique, each total human being is unique. Physically, emotionally, relationally, psychologically—we are each special as we play out the drama of life by our own unique plots. God loves it that way.

This is why Jesus encounters no two people in the same way. He creatively connects with the uniqueness of each new human being. If we treat people with a one-size-fits-all approach, we not only show disrespect for each human being's unique personhood, but we actually show contempt for the gracious creativity of God. Think about it!

Gifts Differ

Jesus understood well that *each person in the family of God has been given his or her own unique set of gifts and capabilities.* He illustrated this when, to get a rest break, He crossed the Sea of Galilee and a huge crowd followed Him. When Jesus climbed the hillside and sat down with His disciples, He saw that huge crowd approaching and asked Philip, "Where shall we buy bread for these people?" Actually, Jesus already had a plan. He saw in that circle of people gathered around Him on the hillside a variety of gifts. Watch Jesus draw them out!

Philip protested, "Eight months' wages wouldn't buy enough bread to feed this crowd." Philip apparently had *treasury gifts.* Maybe he was a CPA, his mind quick with numbers: "Here's the average income. Here is the size of the crowd. Here is the price of bread. Clickety, clickety, click! Conclusion: Eight months' wages wouldn't feed them."

We may be tempted to chide Philip, to accuse him of caring more about figures than about people, that balanced columns meant more than full stomachs. But wherever Christians team up to do a project, accountant's gifts are needed. So, before you criticize the guy who always tracks the numbers to the bottom line, remember: God gave him that gift! God knew groups need balance between the accountants, who "think in columns," and the visionaries, who, although they are indispensable, are also sometimes impractical. True, some bean-counters can't see people. But visionaries sometimes do damage in the long run because some tend to lose touch with the financial facts of life. No matter how bright and grand the vision of ministry, more people get blessed longer when the Philips keep good numbers. Philip had *treasury* gifts.

Another person in that circle around Jesus offered a unique gift. Andrew, Simon Peter's brother, piped up, "Here's a boy with some bread and fish. Maybe that would do." Andrew has *helping gifts*. His heart cares, always searching for ways to help. He thinks, "There's got to be some way we can solve this problem. This boy's sandwich and sardines at least make a start." Sounds pretty impractical from an accountant's standpoint. A can of sardines and a couple of biscuits to feed a convention center full of people! But Andrew didn't throw in the towel just because he couldn't yet see where all the money was coming from. Andrew's perspective was, "We've got to start somewhere!" *Helping gifts*. Without the Andrews in our midst, the accountants sometimes scare off all kinds of ministry. Without the Andrews, the Philips can kill the project by quoting the price!

A third key person sat in Jesus' circle that day. He had *sharing gifts*. His name isn't even mentioned. He's merely "the boy with the fish and the bread." The boy didn't have much. He probably hadn't much experience counting multitudes. He'd likely never even fed a small group, let alone a mob! That morning, the lad may have asked his mother for a lunch to take on his hike in the hills. But when he saw the hungry people, his sharing heart said, "Here's my lunch. It's not much, but you're welcome to it." The boy exercised the gift of generosity.

Creative Collaboration

Then John the apostle specifically explains that Jesus asked the people to sit down on the grass in companies and personally passed out the bread and fish. Somehow, when God's fingers touch them, even the meager gifts offered out of our insufficiency can meet the needs of multitudes.

Jesus is not only available and sensitive and helpful, but He is also *creative*, and not just with the gifts of that little band of helpers on the hillside long ago. He still uses a variety of gifts to accomplish His purposes today. He still "gifts" us when He calls us to work His plans.

Gifts in the Bible

What does the Bible say about gifts that are given to Christians? First, the Lord gives His gifts for a specific purpose. In Ephesians 4:8 and 11, Scripture says that Jesus "gave gifts to men." He gifted "some to be apostles, some to be prophets, some to be evangelists, and some to be pastors and teachers." Notice: Only *some* have teaching gifts. James says,

"Not many of you should presume to be teachers" (James 3:1). Only *some*, evangelists. Only *some*, pastors. Only *some*. But these leadership gifts were given "to prepare God's people for works of service" (Eph. 4:12). Why? *The purpose of gifts is to build up the body of Christ.* Gifts are given to nurture strong relationships, solid character, effective ministry, and rich Christ-likeness. That's what Jesus wants. He always gives His gifts for "the good of others" (1 Cor. 10:24) and "so that the body of Christ may be built up" (Eph. 4:12). Gifts are not for our own pleasure or power.

Jesus hasn't stopped gifting His people. In fact, the apostle Peter said, "Each one should use whatever gift he has received to serve others, faithfully administering God's grace in its various forms" (1 Peter 4:10). Here, Peter describes two forms of gifts. First, "If anyone speaks, he should do it as one speaking the very words of God" (1 Peter 4:11a). Second, "If anyone serves, he should do it with the strength God provides" (1 Peter 4:11b). God gives His words for teaching gifts, His strength for serving gifts.

Note: Teaching gifts are no more "spiritual" than serving gifts. A gifted teacher must not discount other non-teaching gifts: "Truly spiritual Christians study the Bible and pray—like I do!" Nor can Christians with serving gifts regard teachers as less Christian because they "merely talk" instead of "getting their hands dirty doing service." God gave both kinds of gifts. And *every* gift is needed.

Some specific gifts are mentioned in Scripture:

If a man's gift is prophesying, let him use it in proportion to his faith. If it is serving, let him serve; if it is teaching, let him teach; if it is encouraging, let him encourage; if it is contrib-

uting to the needs of others, let him give gener-
ously; if it is leadership, let him govern diligently;
if it is showing mercy, let him do it cheerfully.

(Rom. 12:6–8)

We are not all wired the same way, but we are to
use whatever unique capability God has given us for
the upbuilding of all. That's what gifts are for—not to
build up a person's ego, prestige, or following.

Of course, my giftedness in one area does not
absolve me from service outside of my gift. I have
met some believers who use the whole idea of
spiritual gifts as a cop-out. For example, Harry has
been a Christian for years and has still not identified his gift, consequently he has never consistently
served anybody. "I just don't know what my gift is."
Harry needs to serve others before he will discover
what his gift is. As he serves, his "gift" will become
obvious.

Every player on the baseball team has to hit the
ball. But not everybody is Jose Canseco. So Canseco
is a designated hitter. Every player occasionally has
to throw the ball or be charged with an error. But not
everyone is Nolan Ryan. That's why he's on the
mound. Each player wears a glove because sooner or
later he'll have to catch the ball. But not everybody
catches behind home plate. But while every player
occasionally hits, catches, and throws, the coach
organizes the team positions around each player's
unique gift.

Just so in the Christian enterprise; although servant-heartedness is for every Christian, at times,
each of us may be called to serve outside our unique
area of giftedness.

My Place in the Plan

There is no task in the body I shouldn't be willing to try at one time or another. If the ball is hit to me, I need to give it my best. I want to meet needs that fall in my path—whether I'm particularly gifted to meet them or not. But when backing off to prioritize my energies, to plan my calendar, to identify my calling, I must design my commitment to fit my gift. If not, I may allow myself to be railroaded into tasks that only make me miserable and nonproductive, while finding no time to play the position God assigned to me on His team.

Dangerous Recruiters

Beware of guilt-motivating zealots who think up programs, then recruit square pegs into round holes to keep their programs running. Beware of signals like, "If you don't teach Sunday school, then you don't love kids." Or "Those who really love the unchurched will join my witnessing class." If I push my pet project and gobble up "recruits" whether gifts fit tasks or not, I am not treating people the way Jesus treats people. I may even be thwarting God's plans, and, in the larger picture, gifts will be wasted.

The body won't grow unless *each* person does the work for which God designed him or her. *Every person*—not just some persons—must use his or her gift! "From him the whole body . . . grows and builds itself up . . . *as each part does its work*" (Eph. 4:16, emphasis mine). The body of Christ has no extra, dispensable, vestigial organs.

Peter and Paul both clearly say, "Use your gifts to serve the body." God gives to every church all the gifts needed to do what God expects that church to do. He probably does not expect a community of believers to be doing things for which He has not supplied the gifts. But when each Christian in the Body has identified his or her gift and is using that gift faithfully, the result is not only powerfully effective, but morale-building and fulfilling to each person.

When Each Part Works

Stephanie and Teena had never met each other, even though they lived in the same apartment complex and worked only thirteen floors apart. They lived in two very different worlds. Stephanie, a Christian, worked on the fourteenth floor as a legal secretary. Teena was a friendly but thoroughly secular person who worked as a cocktail waitress in the mezzanine bar. Then came that "energy crunch" back in the seventies. Stephanie and Teena began car-pooling from their suburban apartment complex to their downtown office building. Thus began a close friendship between them.

Some months into their friendship, Teena questioned Stephanie, "What is it that's so different about you? You seem to trust people. You expect good things to happen. You have such neat friends and lots of them. The gals from your office say you never bad-mouth anybody, not even the boss. And they tell me you always pull more than your share of work. You trust men. What's your secret?"

Stephanie stammered at first. "Well, er, I don't want to sound like a 'holy Joe' or anything . . . but if you see good stuff in my life . . . it's likely because I'm a Christian."

"So what's a Christian?"

"It's a . . . someone who follows Jesus Christ."

"How do you get to be one?"

"Well, I . . . I don't know exactly how to tell you. But if you have some time Thursday night, come over for dinner and I'll invite Sandra, too. She's the one who explained it to me. She can explain it to you."

So Sandra, who has gifts of evangelism, taught Teena how to become a Christian. Teena accepted Christ. For the Sunday night of her baptism, she sent out silver embossed invitations to all of her friends, mostly clientele at the bar. Teena was streetwise and tough, but likeable, too. So her friends said, "Hey, if it's for Teena, whatever it is—hog-killing, bar mitzvah, birthday, baptism—we'll be there."

And they came. Six pews full! Joking about the roof caving in because they were in church.

However, another Christian friend, Jennifer, who had gifts of hospitality, also sent out silver invitations to Teena's guest list, inviting them all to Jennifer's house for a reception in honor of Teena after the baptism. They also invited Sandra. And Stella who had teaching gifts, and Fred with gifts of encouragement. Plus others.

All Teena's guests went from the baptism to the reception. God worked in this "gift mix" so that over the next year and a half, more than a dozen of Teena's friends accepted Jesus and sent out silver embossed invitations to their baptisms, followed by Jennifer's receptions.

Questions: Who actually won Teena and her friends to Christ? Should Stephanie feel guilty because she was not the one who actually taught Teena? Did Sandra fail because she didn't actually baptize her? When the rest became Christians, did Jennifer and the gang feel left out because they neither witnessed, evangelized, or baptized? Of course not! In Jesus' plan, every one of these Christians played well his or her role in this soul-winning drama. Each exercised his or her own gift in a synergism that met the needs of each new Christian at just the right time. And each found fulfillment in doing what God designed him or her to do.

Jesus sat on a hill with His circle of followers gathered around Him. He drew out the unique gift of each one—blended with the gifts of all to do His Kingdom business. He still does it that way today. Where every Christian functions by gift, God does His Kingdom business.

Focus:

1. What do you enjoy doing in the Lord's kingdom? Is that your gift?
2. Have you felt God's leading toward other gifts? How do you know? What do these nudgings feel like?
3. Do you know your own spiritual gift? How do/did you discover it?

Now look at what He's gotten us into. We kids never could figure out our oldest brother.

Mom and Dad told strange stories about the night He was born. As early as twelve He wasn't exactly normal. At times He seemed a bit touched in the head. Then at other times He held us spellbound. He did some amazing things. Miracles, actually. Drew huge crowds everywhere. And the things He said! We were mystified and scared to death. But since He set the whole countryside buzzing, we were all proud of Him. And we enjoyed the attention that spilled over onto us. He seemed headed for the top.

Earlier this week we tried to bring Him with us to the festival. "Everybody that is anybody will be there," we told Him. "Sure, it's a religious gathering. But it's also a public relations bonanza." And our brother had the stuff to blow the doors off this crowd of big shots. We just knew this would be His big break. Walk in and wow this bunch, and the whole nation would be eating out of His hand. And ours. So we told Him, "Here's Your big chance. You'll never amount to much hanging around this dump. Take Your tricks to the city, now, at festival time. Show Your stuff."

But He rattled off some riddle and stayed behind.
So now He shows up in the middle of a mad crowd.
No bodyguards. And no miraculous tricks? And lis-
ten to Him. Can you believe what He is saying to
those big shots? Doesn't He know who they are?
Why, that loony brother of ours is liable to . . . that is
. . . He might actually get Himself killed.

I'm outa here. . . .

8

The Strength of Vulnerability

His brothers thought Jesus needed to be brought up to speed in the science of public relations. He was too timid, too camera-shy. He spent too much time alone. He didn't know how to set up a photo opportunity. He didn't see the power of pulling strings. He didn't drop names, kiss babies, or polish apples. His timing was off, His stage presence dull. He lacked tact. He didn't know how to play the crowd, manipulate the media, or grab headlines. He didn't seem to understand that if you're going to be a winner, you've got to *operate from a position of strength.*

So Jesus' brothers decided to coach Him a bit. A feast day

Finding Power Where You Least Expect It

was coming. A great opportunity for a superstar to shine and strut. Lots of people. Lots of action. The network cameras would be rolling, and a man on His way to the top couldn't afford to pass up a chance like this.

"You ought to leave here and go to Judea, so that your disciples may see the miracles you do. No one who wants to become a public figure acts in secret. Since you are doing these things, show yourself to the world" (John 7:3–4).

In other words, "C'mon, brother! Operate from a position of strength! Flex Your muscles. Flash Your pearly whites. Razzle-dazzle 'em, Jesus. That's the way to win the world."

Sounds familiar, right? Don't we still say that you need your hand on the throttle if you're going to move down the track? You need to know which buttons to push and which arms to twist. It is very possible that if Jesus were here today we would give Him the same advice. Can you imagine one of our political handlers or celebrity managers giving Jesus a few pointers?

"To begin with, Jesus, You've got to get out of this one-horse town. You'll never get anywhere with Jerusalem as Your base. It's too ethnically typecast and primitive. We'll get You to Rome. Work on Your accent. Get You some new clothes (heaven knows You could use them). We'll build You a whole new image.

"And these guys You hang out with? They stay here. There isn't much room in the Roman power structure for a bunch of hicks who smell like fish. We'll round up some guys who'll give You some class.

"One other thing: If there's any truth to this stuff about being born in a stable, play that down. It hurts Your credibility.

"We've got a lot of work to do, Jesus. A lot of polishing and shining. By the way, have You ever heard of Madison Avenue? Neilsen ratings? George Gallup? Sound bytes? Letterman and Larry King Live?"

Jesus' Vulnerability

The reason Jesus' brothers wanted Jesus to operate from a position of strength is clear: Scripture says "his own brothers did not believe" (John 7:5). You mean, they were atheists? Well, no, they were *religious*, all right. No doubt they believed God existed. But they didn't understand that God came into our world to be a *servant* and to finally go to a cross.

John 5:44 hits this same point with a hammer blow: "How can you believe if you accept praise from one another, yet make no effort to obtain the praise that comes from the only God?" To believe is to give glory to God. As long as we aim to be glorified by people, we don't really believe in God. We believe in ourselves. And when push comes to shove, whatever gets us praise (votes? prestige? success?) will override our desire to please God.

Thus a fundamental flaw in the brothers' assumptions warps their counsel: "If you want to become a public figure. . . ." Jesus had no desire to be a public figure. Where did Jesus' brothers get that idea? The kind of Messiah they believed in was not the Messiah Jesus would be. This may surprise you, but Jesus wasn't trying to impress people. His agenda was not visibility, fame, or clout. That's why His approach bewildered His brothers. The Lord Jesus operated from a position of vulnerability, even of weakness. No puffed-up Madison Avenue image here.

With Jesus, what folks saw is what they got. He presented His genuine self with His true feelings. There is not a hint in the New Testament of Jesus putting up a front. He never disguised, nor capitalized upon, His humble birth. He was never embarrassed to be seen with, nor tried to sanctify, His mother. He didn't demand that people call Him Rabbi or Teacher. He wasn't too dignified to play with children or too holy to eat with the pimps and prostitutes on the other side of the tracks. He didn't jockey for the head table, nor was He the first to roar away from a traffic light.

Authoritative Authenticity

One word describes the way that others perceived Jesus as He walked among people. *Authentic.* He was accused of being a lot of things, but never accused of not being Himself. In fact, to the contrary, people were amazed at how genuine and candid He was.

Some suggest that vulnerability and Christianity don't mix. A Christian should always maintain his or her dignity, they contend. Christians should never show their emotions lest they appear soft. Camouflage your weaknesses. Present your best profile. Don't allow yourself to get into a situation where you come off looking silly. Always be in charge of yourself and in control of the situation. Never let 'em see you sweat!

Can you imagine our Lord hiding His emotions in order to impress the crowds? No. But you can imagine Him removing His clothes and washing the apostles' feet. You can imagine Him brushing away a tear with one hand while touching a leper with the other. You can imagine Him burying His face in His hands in front of Lazarus' tomb. And you can imagine Him red-faced and furious as He roars through the tables of the money-changers.

That is authenticity.

The picture of authenticity is always painted in earthy tones, and I picture Jesus in these colors: a log cabin brown shade of honesty; green simplicity, bright and springish; sincerity in a tone of sunset gold that invites friendship; an ocean blueness of acceptance that brings memories of a cool breeze of salty air.

Genuineness doesn't need glitzy neon colors that flash with overstatement and disguise. There is no need for blistering yellows or roaring purples to cover up the real self. Courageous authenticity allows a person to stand alone. Crutches made of professions, possessions, and designer clothes are thrown out; the real person remains. No games. No charades. No fronts.

However, these days glitz markets better than genuineness, advertising better than authenticity. Dean Martin comments on the way he has seen the glitz of Hollywood impact American culture: "Everything is a sham, a racket, from sex to singing to cultural respectability. You're born, you die, and in between you somehow delude yourself into thinking some of it means something."[13]

A lot of people see it Dean Martin's way. Maybe that's why it's so refreshing to meet someone who is not obsessed with impressing you, who isn't trying to manipulate you. We just feel better when we know someone whose self-image isn't wrapped up in what he or she drives or who he or she knows or what he or she owns, much less in who he or she controls, whose interest in you isn't self-serving.

People felt that way when they encountered Jesus. They might not have agreed with Him; they may not have understood Him. But they could never say they weren't given the unvarnished truth about Him or by Him.

Will the Real Jesus Please Stand

Years later when Jesus' friend John was old, the first words of his letter reminded his readers how authentic Jesus was: "That which was from the beginning, which we have heard, which we have seen with our eyes, which we have looked at and our hands have touched—this we proclaim concerning the Word of life" (1 John 1:1).

"We have seen God!" John declares. "He has been here among us and we have seen Him. God didn't disguise Himself in bright lights nor did He hide on a mountain. He was in our midst. He wore diapers. He burped. He sweated. He ate with us. He talked our language. And we touched Him."

That is why Jesus didn't take His brothers' advice. It wasn't His style. It wasn't who He was and *is!* It went against the nature of Jesus to be anything but Himself. He was more interested in relationship with us than intimidation over us.

So instead of roaring off to the Jerusalem feast in a limousine surrounded by hoopla and flag waving, He waited. He waited until He could slip in quietly. No trumpets. No fanfare. He didn't announce His presence and then bolster it with, "I'm the fellow who did those miracles, walked on water, and fed the five thousand, so you better listen up." No. He walked in a side door and simply began to teach. (Some of the people listening didn't even know who He was!)

He made Himself totally available, even to the enemy. What's more, He spoke inflammatory words without the protection of any prestigious group behind Him, with no bodyguards around Him. He even asked, "Why are you trying to kill Me?" Jesus made Himself completely vulnerable. That is how He operated. The prophets said He would.

He had no beauty or majesty to attract us to him,
 nothing in his appearance that we should
 desire him.
He was despised and rejected by men,
 a man of sorrows, and familiar with suffering.
Like one from whom men hide their faces
 he was despised, and we esteemed him not.
(Isa. 53:2-3)

So Jesus made Himself vulnerable that feast day
in the temple. He operated from a position of weakness, not of strength. And He calls us to follow! To
deny self, take up a cross, and follow!

Imitators of His Style

Jesus personally walked a vulnerable road, but He
taught His friends to walk that way as well.

The apostle Paul picked up on this, "Christ Jesus
came into the world to save sinners—of whom I am
the worst" (1 Tim. 1:15). That was not merely Paul's
technique. Nor was it a communication device contrived to diminish the talking distance between himself and "ordinary mortals." This was Paul's genuine
lifestyle, his honest estimate of himself. He refused to
pretend he was something more, simply to gain ad-
vantages or credibility.

Listen again to Paul: "When I came to you, brothers, I did not come with eloquence or superior wisdom . . . " (1 Cor. 2:1). Now watch this: "I came to you
in weakness and fear, and with much trembling. My
message and my preaching were not with wise and
persuasive words, but with a demonstration of the
Spirit's power, so that your faith might not rest on
men's wisdom, but on God's power" (1 Cor. 2:3-5).
And Paul's vulnerability was his strength! From a

human standpoint, defeated, in prison, under a death penalty, Paul transformed the world.

Or consider Peter. If anyone had a reason for some boasting, Peter did. Skim his résumé:

- Three years of personal training under the Son of God
- Personal friend of Jesus
- Witness of the Transfiguration, events in the Garden of Gethsemane, and the Crucifixion
- Walked on water
- Received the gift of speaking in other languages
- Personally commissioned by God to carry the gospel into all parts of the world
- Worker of various miracles and cures
- Testimony of visions
- Writer of two New Testament letters

Some bio, huh? Can you imagine a long-ball hitter like that being introduced to speak at a Christian conference? My, the introduction would crowd the message off the clock! That kind of experience should be broadcast loudly in order to enhance credibility, right? Apparently not for Peter! When the opportunity came to list off his qualifications, he chose not to. His simple self-introduction reads: "Simon Peter, a servant and apostle of Jesus Christ" (2 Peter 1:1).

Hedging His Bet

On the other hand, if you follow the advice of the power brokers, you'll quickly learn that it is booby-trapped with weaknesses. Are we modern North

American believers developing the nasty habit of depending on our own power and talents in spite of Jesus' warning?

> You know that the rulers of the Gentiles lord it over them, and their high officials exercise authority over them. Not so with you. Instead, whoever wants to become great among you must be your servant, and whoever wants to be first must be your slave—just as the Son of Man did not come to be served, but to serve, and to give his life as a ransom for many.
>
> (Matt. 20:25–28)

Cover-up

This lack of integrity easily infects Christians, too. The "show 'em your stuff" mentality sometimes overflows into the church. In fact, one of the rarest places to find authenticity is among God's people. Before you dismiss such a brash statement, consider some clues to our "position of strength," "project a good image," and "never let 'em see you sweat" mentality.

First, we tend to *cover our flaws*. We dress sharp. We smell good. Plastic smiles sparkle in our church pews. Neat leather Bibles lie open on laps. We nod at the right places, stand at the right moments, and bow at the appropriate times. My, we look nice.

But how many broken hearts beat painfully beneath our new suits? How much guilt and anxiety are camouflaged by mascara?

If we dressed like we felt, how many would come to church in new clothes? In all probability, very few. Many would come clothed in white hospital robes, peeling off bandages, baring our wounds for treatment. Or draped in mourning clothes. Still others might even sit in sackcloth and ashes.

Real spiritual healing comes only through this kind of honesty: "Confess your sins to each other and pray for each other so that you may be *healed*" (James 5:16, emphasis mine).

The church is strongest when it rings truest. Can you imagine cute pep rally songs in the catacomb assemblies of the first century? Did the leaders, stumbling through dark corridors, carrying candles in their hands, spend much time on their "clerical image" or public relations strategies for moving to a "position of strength"? Can you envision the apostles talking religious babble and wearing pompous clergy clothes?

No. Christianity roared across the civilized world because of integrity, not image. The best growth rates were the years without legal recognition or social clout. Even years of persecution. Why? Because God blessed authentic faith! Then, after the Edict of Constantine, when the Church received legal status and began to jockey for the support of political power, the Christian movement began to lose its steam.

Charisma

Second, we sometimes rely on "ministry by charisma." We want preachers that can "wow" the audience. Let Christ be represented by a real charmer, someone who can bring in the crowds and excite the masses. Now, there is nothing wrong in utilizing God-given gifts of communication. But there is something wrong, even idolatrous, in replacing God's Holy Spirit with the force of human personality, or scholarship, or reputation, or. . . .

Position

Third, we sometimes operate as if we expect kingdom growth through political posturing. We want to headline Christians who can impress. Wouldn't it be great if the governor was a part of our church? Wouldn't it be something if we could get a movie star to testify at our services? Or how about a converted porno publisher?

In Canada, the premier of the province lived in our city, and we got to know him and his family. I'd wake up in the night, fantasizing that the premier of British Columbia might become part of our new little church plant. I'd think, what a boost that would give us! I must really be something.

The truth is, all people need the gospel. And God doesn't need just the "influential" to carry His message. If He has succeeded in communicating through donkeys and tornadoes, He can probably use ordinary Joes like us. And what spiritual benefit would there be in joining a church simply because the premier was a member of it?

Scholarship

Fourth, some of us may occasionally be guilty of intimidation by information as we go out to blow away people with the Bible. We may fire off our barrage of biblical bullets from six feet above criticism, quoting our repertoire of verses and packaged answers ready-made for any situation. We anticipate objections, ask leading questions, and close with strong emotion. We "sell" Jesus. Either the poor intimidated soul will have to say yes to our pitch, or he won't have anything left to say yes with. And even if this "works," there is a vast difference between low sales resistance and a holy hunger for God.

Professionalism

Fifth, we will always feel tempted to trust in religious professionalism. Manipulation. Climbing the ecclesiastical ladder is no longer merely a workout routine for church leaders, but has become an aggressive race. Titles, credentials, speaking invitations, growth statistics, books published become toeholds to higher rungs. And the crowd marvels at "how mightily God is using Brother Big-Shot," while at the same time, many in the crowd feel personally useless to Christ because they themselves are so "ordinary" by comparison.

All of these power moves work together to create a dense and intimidating network of *professionalism* in the church. Positions and achievements lead decision-makers farther away from the people in the streets, imprisoning these "professionals" in offices, conference rooms, libraries, and airplanes. The usefulness of some once-effective servants is being strangled by clerical collars and cluttered calendars.

The difference between the prophet in the Bible and the professional in the limelight dangerously resembles the difference between authentic Christianity and insincerity. Professionalism runs counter to the heart of Jesus' words in Matthew 23:8, "You have only one Master." I am deeply troubled to notice that the more professional I long to be, the more artificial I become.

Possibly prophets are needed more urgently than professionals—prophets who deny themselves, rather than professionals who exalt themselves; prophets who are weak rather than professionals who are polished; prophets who may get stoned rather than professionals who get pampered; prophets walking with Christ, who hunger for God in prayer and who weep over sins. Prophets! Not more slick professionals with Teflon exteriors that slough the messy, painful side of life.

An authentic walk with Christ makes us hunger for God in prayer and weep over sins. God draws us toward the holiness of heaven. Is there professionalism in that?

The Vulnerability of Strength

Such a pose is impossible to hold for very long. And it only intimidates those who buy in. It impedes intimacy and definitely inspires no one. Even more importantly, it isn't Jesus' style!

Do you sense the liabilities? A first vulnerability, or weakness, of strength is this: When we hold any kind of power over another person (be it physical, positional, or even psychological), we *find it difficult to trust the genuineness of our relationship with that person.* I never really know how authentic my relationship is with anyone who stands in awe of me or fears me or is beholden to me or wants to use me. A wealthy friend once confided in a moment of candor: "I never know for sure who my real friends are because everybody fawns over me and then wants something." Only in vulnerability and openness do we really know where we stand; only then can we trust a relationship to be authentic.

The second: When I operate from a position of power over someone, even a psychological advantage, I *rob that individual of personhood.* I subtly (sometimes not so subtly) diminish that person's significance and make him merely a component of my sphere of influence. God doesn't operate that way! Jesus came as a servant, and He died on a cross.

Third: *idolatry*. God gets dethroned and we take charge.

Fourth: Ultimately operating from positions of strength leads to depletion and then, even destruction. We saw this happen in the 1992 elections. A former Texas State Railroad Commissioner, Mrs. Lena Guerrero, who began her campaign with a strong lead and had done a good job at her previous State appointment, lost the race dismally. Why? Because, if the news about her was accurate, she had pretended to have graduated from the University of Texas and to have been a member of Phi Beta Kappa honor scholastic society. But the truth came out that she hadn't graduated at all. In fact, she had flunked a number of courses, including Mexican Americans in the Southwest, Texas Legislature, and Readings in Government![14] Apparently she couldn't resist the temptation to present an image larger than life. Few people can, especially in the public arena. Why? They feel it essential to operate from a position of more strength than they really believe they have!

Jesus did not teach professional childlikeness, nor professional tenderheartedness.

Pause and think for a minute. How are you perceived by those who know you well? Would you fit the description of a prophet or a professional? Are you authentic or artificial? Ponder these questions:

- Do I try to project more strength or claim more power than I really have?
- Do I feel a need to communicate personal achievements in order to be a legitimate and comfortable player in a relationship?

- Do people around me feel that I will listen to them if they have a problem?
- What percentage of my time am I available to anyone who wants to talk to me?
- How many people would say that they were genuinely served by me in the last few days?

The Strength of Vulnerability

What about the strength of vulnerability? Operating from a position of vulnerability promises a number of powerful pluses.

- Vulnerability promotes honesty, thus
- vulnerability inspires trust, thus
- vulnerability lowers defenses, thus
- vulnerability melts hostility, thus
- vulnerability puts a listener at ease.
- And when we relinquish our "position of strength," we become more teachable ourselves.

That's how Jesus functioned. Write this in stone: *Authentic Christianity creates abiding faith.* The real thing may not create any initial flashing lights and blasting trumpets, but the long-term results are enormously substantial: personal faith that can stand alone, free of crutches, makeup, or razzle-dazzle. The result is an obedient trust in Jesus and nothing else.

What a phony idea to think that we need something bigger than reality to do God's work. The world sets the agenda for the professional man, but the spiritual person follows God's agenda. The new wine of Jesus bursts the old wineskins of professionalism. We don't need professionalism; we need a holy hunger for God.

How to Get Real

How does one become more authentic? If I have become too plastic in my relationships, what can I do?

The answer is almost too simple. First, put simply, authenticity is the result of an unquenchable love for the Lord. Authenticity appears most fully in those whom life has genuinely broken, and this is disturbing. Think about it.

If one loves Jesus with his or her *whole* heart, what room is left for selfish love? None. If there is no room left for self, then there is no need for self-promotion. The more we love the Master the less we are concerned about self and the more authentic we are. The more we are consumed with presenting the Savior, the less we feel the need to present ourselves.

Authenticity is refreshing. We can relax from the mad scramble to cover for our mistakes. We need no longer feel stressed by our compulsion to impress people with our achievements because we realize that anything we have achieved is trash in comparison with God's gift. We feel no burden to drive the best or wear the latest because our self-image ultimately comes from *God's* assessment of us, not other people's.

Authenticity, then, is a fruit of full relationship with Jesus. But full relationship with Christ is always a direction we are heading, not a level at which we have arrived. And accountability to Christ-like people aids progress toward full devotion to Jesus. Paradoxically: Possibly the most authentic I can be is to honestly admit my inauthenticity to my fellow believers and ask them to help by monitoring my progress and confronting me on it when they see a need to.

The Cost of Credibility

Second, authenticity will never be available unless we are willing to pay the price. Yes, vulnerability means we may get taken advantage of, even hurt deeply. Jesus did. That is why He is called the "man of sorrows, and familiar with suffering" (Isa. 53:3).

We shouldn't be surprised that Christians sometimes hurt. At an earlier stage of my Christian walk, I believed Christians *might* suffer deep hurt by practicing servant-heartedness. I am now firmly convinced that it is *inevitable* that authentic servants will get hurt. In fact, suffering is the very means by which some of the most significant "peopling" gets done. Dr. James Dittes calls ministry "grief work." In *When the People Say No*, he wrote,

To grieve is to take two coffee cups from the cupboard in the morning, only to remember that one's wife is dead or separated . . . and to have to put the cup back. . . . To grieve is to wake up on a brilliant sunny morning with spontaneous, unbidden anticipation of playing golf, only to be reminded instantly by heavy limbs that one has had a stroke . . . and to close one's eyes, now moist. . . . To grieve is to pour one's energies for months and years into the struggle of a beleaguered minority group or a beleaguered marriage or a beleaguered teenager—standing by patiently and wisely and lovingly, and indeed making a crucial difference—only to have the group or couple or teenager, having found themselves, shun you as a threatening enemy. Other people may experience only a few times in a long lifetime the grief of losing a crucial partner; the grief of a crucial promise broken by a parent (or a teacher) absolutely trusted until then; the grief of being jilted by a lover, divorced by a spouse, betrayed by a friend.[15]

But a genuine ministering Christian experiences many such moments of grief. Indeed we may frequently experience all of these in the course of only one week. That's okay. Jesus did.

The Man of Sorrows, acquainted with grief, operated on my soul and yours by totally allowing Himself to be hated and rejected and killed. But sometimes there's joy and laughter at the bottom of a broken heart.

Three Words

We don't hear much out of Jesus' brothers after they gave Jesus their pep talk on public relations. And were it not for three special words written by Luke, the end of their story would remain a mystery.

But Luke fills us in on the outcome with just three words, three words that can easily pass unnoticed. Yet they drive home the payoff of authenticity. Get your pen poised because you'll want to underline them.

You'll find them in the first chapter of Acts, verse 14. Luke has just listed the names of those who watched Jesus ascend to heaven, then gathered together to pray. Friends get first billing: Peter, John, James, and the other apostles. Of course, Mary, too. Then Luke says: "They all joined together constantly in prayer, along with the women and Mary the mother of Jesus, *with his brothers*" (emphasis mine).

There they are. The same ones who tried to coach Jesus into the winner's circle; who tried to position

Him for power; the same ones who wanted to help Jesus get to the top. They have seen Him finally front and center—hanging on a cross. Totally vulnerable. Totally helpless. But totally in control and totally victorious. The same brothers who didn't believe in Him now believe!

Focus:

1. Why didn't Jesus want to impress people with His style? How should we follow His example?
2. In what ways has the "show 'em your stuff" mentality come into the church? Into your life?
3. Do you feel more like a prophet or a professional? Why?
4. What does "strength in vulnerability" mean to you? Do you have it? How can you cultivate it?
5. Is there a situation you're facing now in which you have pretended strength? How would vulnerability be a better way? Why?

Aren't all men interested in the same thing? Not that I minded, of course. Until, until that horrible, wonderful day. I guess my lover and I should have expected to be caught, in the middle of the day and all. But that never crossed my mind until the door burst open and these high and mighty types from down around the temple pulled me right out of what's-his-name's arms and dragged me out the door with scarcely time to grab my coat.

Then they forced me into that circle of gawking men. They stopped and looked around for the carpenter, then shoved me right up in His face. At first, I couldn't bear to raise my head, but when I finally looked into His eyes, He looked back at me in that strange way, totally different from the way any man had ever looked at me up close before.

Then, everybody was shouting at once, demanding that this strange carpenter pass the sentence of adultery on me. At first, I was utterly humiliated. Then when I realized they had deliberately left my man behind, I felt roaring mad. But both humiliation and anger froze into terror when I heard, "Stone her until she is dead."

What happened next is a blur. The carpenter said nothing. Just knelt and started writing with His finger in the dirt. The crowd kept demanding that He sentence me. He stood again and looked at them, in that same strange way He first looked at me. Then He spoke something softly to them and knelt again. I closed my eyes and braced myself for the first stone to bite my flesh. A strange tense silence fell over the crowd, except for the sound of shoes on gravel. Nothing happened.

Eternity passed. When I finally opened my eyes, to my astonishment everyone had left but the carpenter. He was looking at me. When most men had looked at me in recent years, I felt naked, as if they were mentally undressing me. But never had I felt as bare as now. No, not physically naked. This was no lustful leer. Oh, no. The compassion in the carpenter's eyes gently laid bare my soul. I thought I saw His tears . . . and for the first time in forever I felt decent.

Even though just minutes earlier I had been inflamed with lust and the crowd had been inflamed with hatred, the carpenter looked at me and at them in this strange way . . .. and all of us felt hope!

9

Fight for People

How would you like to listen to a kettledrum solo for a couple of hours? Boom, boom, boom! A few minutes? Okay, but even the best of musicians can only get so much variety out of this mama of the percussion instruments. "No!" you say, "give me two hours with the soaring soprano of the flute. That would be sweet to the ear." Ahh, now that is music . . . for a while. In fact, there are very few instruments that, played solo, can sustain our interest indefinitely. The long-term attraction of a good orchestra is not in its solos, but in its symphony. Music moves us when it delicately balances sounds, blending, say, the melodious

Striking a Balance Between Forgiving and Condoning

trumpet with the thundering tuba and the compelling clarinet with the subtle strings of the violin.

The balance principle transfers from the concert hall to the kitchen. A delicious meal is essentially a balanced blend of the sweet with the sour, the strong with the subtle, and the predictable with the exotic. A good chef master-mixes ingredients like flour, raw eggs, or lard that by themselves are undesirable, but paired up with the right pan-partners become mouth-watering, finger-licking dishes like, say, strawberry shortcake or pecan pie.

World-class athletes also know the value of balance. They blend strength with style, speed with control, and training with rest. It takes a synchronized spectrum of muscles, coordinated correctly, to throw farther, run faster, or jump higher than the competition and bring home the gold. So a key secret in sports, cuisine, or music is balance.

But to no one is balance more important than to a person attempting to follow Jesus Christ. The wise man knew this when he wrote:

My son, do not forget my teaching,
    but keep my commandments in your heart,
for they will prolong your life many years
    and bring you prosperity.
Let love and faithfulness never leave you. . . .
                         (Prov. 3:1–2, 3a)

Balance

Balance. Balance of law and heart. Balance of mercy and truth. Coordinating praise with correction. Sprinkling doctrine with spontaneity. Knowing when to forgive and when to forsake. That is balance.

Like the conductor, the chef, and the athlete, the Christian needs to crucially balance the ingredients of faith. It's crucial, not just for him or her, but for those near him or her.

The aim of a balanced spiritual life is to treat other people with spiritual balance. But it's tricky. Sometimes we are so bent on being right with God that we misuse people. And sometimes we are so afraid of hurting people that we water down the will of God. Some of us are so bent on truth that we forget mercy, others so tenderhearted that they forget truth.

Tip this delicate spiritual scale and we may tumble headlong into one extreme or another. Traditions begin to outweigh effectiveness or pragmatism upstages biblical truth. Sometimes people get sacrificed on the altar of doctrinal purity, or we give away the store of doctrinal faithfulness in the name of being people-sensitive.

Is balance possible? Is it realistic for us to attempt to treat people with grace and truth?

This question is a key one for churches that are serious about being obedient to the Scriptures. When do you allow divorce and when do you prohibit it? When do you discipline and when do you forgive? When do you overlook sin in the name of patience and when do you confront it in the name of purity? When are we to be held accountable and when do we need empathy?

Watch Jesus' Balancing Act

This is where individual Christians pick up again on the peopling skills of Jesus. Watch His balance as He encounters several kinds of sin and extenuating circumstances in one chapter of Scripture: John 8. The major players in this drama represent the two extremes: religious leaders determined to protect the institution and enforce the law contrasted with a woman in desperate need of grace. Between them stands Jesus. He extends His hands in both directions and offers this principle: *Beware of a view of the law that hurts people. And beware of a view of people that ignores sin.*

The Showdown

The city was just beginning to stir that morning when Jesus descended from the Mount of Olives. Dew moistened the grass, and crowing roosters split the silence. Early risers were leaving their homes and going to work. While merchants opened their shops, children left for school, and blacksmiths fired their forges.

But everywhere you went, the town was buzzing about the strange man from Galilee. Yesterday He had shocked everyone by asserting, "If a man is thirsty, let him come to me and drink. Whoever believes in me, as the Scripture has said, streams of living water will flow from within him" (John 7:38).

Animated controversy broke out, "What kind of man would say such things?"

"He must be a prophet."

"I think He is the Messiah."

"Are you crazy? He is an imposter!"

No wonder, then, that the moment Jesus entered the temple court, a crowd encircled Him. The Master sat down and began to teach.

He was soon interrupted, however, as another crowd erupted into the temple court. It was actually a small mob, an angry mob. They marched with a confident fierceness, eyes burning with a religious fervor. They were elegantly dressed and looked powerful; well-trimmed beards, flowing robes, colorful cords. National leaders. They were the Supreme Court, Vatican, and Congress of the Jewish people. Wealthy and powerful. Not accustomed to sharing the spotlight with anyone, especially a blue-collared carpenter.

How They Saw the Woman

They shoved along a woman, scantily dressed, disheveled, eyes wide with fear. She contrasted starkly to those dragging her through the narrow streets. They were in power, she was the victim. They were many; she was alone. They were self-righteous; she was humiliated, no doubt. She struggled to keep her balance as each arm was squeezed in the grip of a fast-walking Pharisee.

She struggled to gather her thoughts. It had all happened so quickly. The door had flown open so violently it ricocheted off the wall. In they had stormed. She barely had time to grab something to cover her nakedness before being yanked into the street. She noticed that their statements were strangely centered on someone else. "Let's take this one to Him." "We'll show the people the imposter He really is."

We don't know much about the woman. Perhaps she was a young girl who had spent a passionate night with a boyfriend. Or maybe passion was her profession, and some of her accusers were also some of her customers. Or it's possible that she was a good wife simply caught in a "one-time wayward rendezvous." We don't know. But for all we don't know, we do know one thing for sure: She was not the point. She was only a hapless pawn in a vicious power move. The Pharisees had no more desire to help her than they did to kiss a Roman soldier. Their sole desire was to humiliate Jesus, and this woman was their visual aid. They wanted to trap Him, and she was their bait.

How They Saw Jesus

Jesus was a threat. Folks flocked to Him in droves. He had even said their system was going to end. Jesus threatened their position, their money, their prestige, and their power. Threatening their peace of mind, Jesus said things that probed the depths of their hearts. And if they allowed themselves to think about these things too much, they couldn't live with themselves.

Jesus was also a threat because He was reminding people of the purpose of the law. He was reinstating balance. He was demonstrating that any law or doctrine that did not help people grow closer to God was not from God. You can write that in stone, too! *Any would-be application of God's Word that does not have at its end the growth of God's people is actually a misapplication.*

The group stormed through the crowd of listeners, scattering them like doves. The woman was thrown at the seated Nazarene with a torrent of accusations.

"We pulled this woman out of bed with her lover," a sarcastic voice shouted. "The law says to kill her. What would You have us do?"

I imagine the group of Pharisees smiled smugly to each other, proud of their craftiness. They had Him now!

How They Saw the Law

As the woman looked around at her accusers she saw a group of men so consumed by their own agendas that they saw everything and everyone from a distorted perspective.

Above all, this woman's accusers saw the law as "useful." They burned with one passion: Protect their positions in the religious institution. The law served as a useful tool for their purposes. The law they had in mind, however, went beyond God's. It was *their* law: a complicated web of traditions and dictates designed to control people. And what they called "the law" for them was sacred. This complex system had accrued layer by layer for generations. It was the glue that held their socio-religious system together, assuring their security, status, and identity. And at this moment, the law was useful as a means of getting rid of Jesus—or any other formidable threat—in order to maintain control. The law was their shears with which to clip the wings of this upstart Galilean who was getting out of hand.

Now, the actual law of God was something else again. God originally designed His law to regulate the life of human beings for their own greater good and for God's greater glory. Put simply: The law was *for* man, not *against* him. Or, as Jesus pointed out on occasion, "The Sabbath was made for man, not man for the Sabbath" (Mark 2:27). It was meant to expand the quality of life, not diminish it.

"If any of you has a sheep and it falls into a pit on the Sabbath, will you not take hold of it and lift it out? How much more valuable is a man than a sheep!" (Matt. 12:11–12) Again Jesus is saying, "People are everything in God's scale of things."

Jesus was once asked, "What's the biggest commandment?" Jesus answered unequivocally, "Love the Lord your God with all your heart and with all your soul and with all your mind and with all your strength. . . . Love your neighbor as yourself. There is no commandment greater than these" (Mark 12:30–31). The pinnacle of it all is to really love God, and thus to value people. But the Pharisees were not interested in people, especially this one shivering before them.

These accusing Pharisees also held a distorted view of sin. In reality, they saw sin as *inconsequential*; in fact, it was so peripheral that they could not see that their own sin was as great as the woman's. Adultery is disastrous. No question about that. But to dishonor God in the center of your heart, even attempt to use His Law to trap His own Son without any concern for people, has to be infinitely more damaging than even adultery.

Don't miss the point! Whenever you find someone whose favorite pastime is finger-pointing and whose favorite phrase is a thundering "The law of God says . . . " you can be sure of one thing. Some precious person at the other end of that pointing finger is about to get bruised. You can also be sure that somewhere behind all that thunder there lurks, at best, a weak and stale relationship with God, if indeed there is any relationship at all; and at worst, as with this woman's accusers, a twisted view of law, a cheap view of people, and a warped view of God.

I can't afford to imitate the Pharisees, even inadvertently. I must be on guard not to apply God's Word in off-balanced ways nor to use law as a weapon against people. An imbalanced view of God inevitably leads us to treat people in an unbalanced way. How can we avoid this?

Through the Eyes of Jesus

We have surveyed this scene from the eyes of the accusers. Now, turn your attention to Jesus' view of things. As this woman searched around the circle of men, her eyes met no mercy. Only face after face with furrowed brows and hard-set jaws. But when she found the tanned face of Jesus, she saw hope. In His eyes she read not accusation, but acceptance. His expression didn't condemn; it comforted. In His silent glance, she sensed compassion.

Don't miss what happened next. First, note what Jesus *did*, and second, note what He did *not* do.

Off the Hook

First, Jesus diverted attention from the woman. She was on cruel display before the gaping stares of the growing crowd. Jesus' first concern was for her. He didn't argue. He avoided religious discussion about the woman. Rather He knelt down and began to write in the sand. You can imagine all the eyes shifting and heads turning.

"What's He doing?"

"Is He picking up a rock?"

"I think He is praying."

No doubt the woman felt some relief for at least a few moments as she escaped the sea of eyes.

Off the Defensive

Second, Jesus didn't fight back. He might have considered demanding that the woman's lover be brought to trial. Or He could have debated that the law doesn't specify *how* a woman caught in adultery is to be killed (Lev. 20:10). Or He could point out that that law hadn't been enforced for centuries. But He didn't.

He took a far more difficult tack. He wouldn't be seduced into a purposeless theological discussion.

Jesus didn't get defensive because He didn't have anything to defend. He wasn't trying to protect His image or maintain control or score points. Jesus demonstrates for us here how foolish and futile it is to get preoccupied with self-defense. When we're under attack for doing right, the best strategy is to continue to do right and not wade into the quicksand of defensiveness.

Jesus' aim was not to humiliate the woman's assailants, though they well deserved it. Remember, Jesus is always sensitive to people and helpful to people: to *all* people—in this case both the woman and the Pharisees.

This time Jesus is creatively baffling at first. He kneels and writes and doesn't say a word. The leaders don't like Jesus' silence. They keep repeating their question. Eventually Jesus stands and responds simply, "If any one of you is without sin, let him be the first to throw a stone at her" (John 8:7). Then He kneels down again.

Putting the Ball in Their Court

How Jesus resisted the desire to burn these hypocrites on the spot can only be a testimony to His deity. For not only did He not punish or humiliate them, He gave *them* their personhood. "If any one of you . . ." He didn't point his finger and reveal the sins of the accusers one by one. "*You* are having an affair, and *you* cheated your business partner, and *you* haven't said a sincere prayer in a year. . . . " He simply says, "If any one of you is without sin, throw the first rock." And He knelt down again, not even curious to see who would walk away first, not taking down names so He could report them to the authorities.

Jesus knows where He is. So He has a special view of people, including these accusers. In spite of what we don't like about them, they are people, too. Jesus saw that. So rather than put them on the defensive, Jesus creatively puts them on the *reflective*. He left each man to wrestle with his own thoughts.

"What about me?"

"Why am I really here?"

"What right do I honestly have to throw a rock at this woman?"

"What is really going on in my heart? Do I genuinely care about God?"

"Now honestly, what is at the bottom of my resentment?"

"What is it that makes me hate Him like this?"

Maybe some began to reflect, "When I really think about it, instead of killing this carpenter, or whoever He is, I ought to beg Him for help."

No doubt, the older men had met their share of shifty characters, from thugs to theologians and some would-be prophets. And they sensed this man was different. See, over there, a grey-whiskered chin drops to a heaving chest, maybe over here a tear slides down a weathered cheek. A silence settles over the crowd—a strange silence, silence so thick you can cut it with a knife. Finally, we hear the crunch of gravel under foot as one man turns and walks away. Then another. We don't know how long it took the whole crowd to leave, but it must have seemed a century to that worried woman. I can't help but wonder if, on their way out of the circle, any of them glanced into the woman's eyes and whispered, "I'm so sorry"?

When they were gone, Jesus asked, "Where are they?" He hadn't been watching, hadn't been keeping records. Eli, the adulterer, left. Baruch, the liar, too, and Ben. . . .

No, Jesus didn't even watch the direction they walked so He could put a tail on them. He simply was not in the condemning business. "For God did not send his Son into the world to condemn the world, but to save the world through him" (John 3:17).

Jesus knew, too, that permanent change doesn't usually come without self-reflection. We are far more deeply convicted by self-recrimination than by another person's accusations. That's why Jesus dumped the questions back into the Pharisees' laps and left them to sort things out. He set them up for self-inventory. Instead of crossing theological swords, He simply made them think!

John the apostle observes that the older ones walked away first. Perhaps that was because age brings with it a more honest self-appraisal and a keener awareness of frailties. The longer we live, the more we discover how miserably we fail when left to our own devices.

Next Jesus turns His attention to the woman. Again, as always, He is *creative*. In Jesus' final interaction with her we hear the symphonic beauty of balance. He walks the thin line between rebuke and forgiveness. Simultaneously He offers both mercy and correction.

How Jesus Treats Brokenness

It is doubtful that in His earthly ministry our Lord ever faced anyone as transparently vulnerable as was this lady at this moment. Caught in blatant sin. Publicly embarrassed. Terrified for her life. In debt to a stranger who had rescued her. Yet feeling totally at His mercy, not knowing what would happen next.

Like a frightened bird who had fallen out of its nest, she must have quivered as she stood alone, facing the man who held her fate in His hands.

Have you ever stood in a place akin to Jesus' position at that moment? Times come when some person's dark secrets have been revealed to us so he or she stands before us absolutely naked in failure, and we hold nearly absolute power over him or her.

It's not an easy situation to be in.

Someone pours his or her heart out to you, trusting you with intimate confessions. What do you say next? A friend hangs his head and admits cheating on a loving mate. What is your next step? You come home early one day only to find your teenage daughter and her friends smoking pot in the garage. How do you respond? You, an elder in the church, are sitting across the table from the church treasurer who has been caught funneling church money into his business. How do you treat him or her?

My long-time friend Carlos runs a prosperous business. People are naturally drawn to him because he is always a barrel of fun. But Carlos also loves Jesus. In fact, his faith is so contagious that an astonishing percentage of the people who come to work in his offices wind up receiving Christ.

Jan, his bookkeeper, was one of these. Some years back, Jan and her husband, Tom, who was not a believer, hit some rocky times in their marriage. The trouble revolved, as such trouble often does, around finances. They were in debt to their eyeballs.

One afternoon, Carlos was shocked to discover several thousand dollars missing from his business, covered by phoney figures. At first he couldn't believe it was Jan. But the evidence left no other possibility.

I asked Carlos, "What did you do next?"

"Well," Carlos admitted, "first I closed the office door and cried. It really hurt me that Jan would do that."

"And then?"

Carlos told how he called Jan in and confronted her. She didn't deny it for one second. She just began to cry and poured out her marital problems and financial crisis. She had given in to temptation and hoped to get the money replaced before it was found missing. She asked if Carlos had pressed charges and how soon she'd have to clear out her desk. But Carlos explained that there would be no charges. Besides, he said she wasn't being fired. "You are my Christian sister, and I want to help you out of this mess," explained Carlos. "All I want is to know you are sorry, that it won't happen again, and that you will pay the money back."

"But there is no way. Tom and I couldn't begin to borrow that much with our credit like it is," Jan said.

Carlos explained, "You can pay it back, a hundred dollars a month, till it's covered—and no interest."

Jan began to cry again, "But even that is impossible. Each month every penny is already spent before I get my check."

"Sure you can, when you get your raise," Carlos explained. "Starting next week I'm raising your salary by one hundred dollars a month."

"Why would you do that?"

"Because I don't want you crushed. I want to see you changed and happy and walking with Jesus."

Then Jan and Carlos prayed together. Jan continued working in Carlos's office as a trusted employee and a loving follower of Jesus for years.

I think Carlos learned this from Jesus, maybe even from the exact point when Jesus stood facing the lady in John 8.

If ever times call for balance, these times do: times when cheeks are stained by forbidden fruit. And perhaps it was for times like these that the Holy Spirit recorded the final lines of Jesus' conversation with the woman caught in adultery.

Jesus' dirt-writing finger came to a stop. He stood up, looked her in the eye, and spoke three times. A few pivotal words that changed her world and can change yours and mine.

A Word of Acceptance

First, "Does no one condemn you?" His first word was *acceptance*. "No one threw any rocks at you? That means that you aren't the only one who has stumbled." There is something wonderfully liberating in being reminded that "all have sinned and fall short of the glory of God" (Rom. 3:23).

Max Lucado said a friend saw this principle at work on a plane in a busy Midwestern airport. The plane was full. The plane was late departing. The passengers were complaining. Not a good time to be a flight attendant, especially the one who caused the delay by forgetting to order the ice. Finally, after an hour of sitting on the runway, a flight attendant stood before the plane full of disgruntled passengers and explained, "We apologize for the delay. We are late because one of your flight attendants forgot to order the ice for this flight. Because this airline frowns on such irresponsibility, the guilty employee will now stand before you."

The anger of the passengers melted into curiosity as they prepared to watch the public humiliation. This isn't something you see on every flight. Imagine their surprise when the flight attendant turned, put up the microphone, then turned back and stood before the people. *She* was the culprit! She was the cause of the delay! Everyone sat a few seconds in stunned silence, not quite knowing how to react. Then a sensitive passenger began to clap his hands. Another followed suit. Soon everyone was applauding! The honest mistake was overshadowed by the honest confession.

Why did everyone applaud? Because each knew it could easily have been him or her. Everyone had forgotten important things a time or two. And, for this hapless flight attendant, the applause was incredibly liberating; just to be reminded that she wasn't the only person who makes mistakes.

Jesus viewed the woman caught in adultery as a person, too. "Lady, don't you see that you're not alone? You're a human being. You're not a useless piece of garbage because you have sinned. You've probably felt isolated, thinking, 'I'm the only woman in the world like this. I must be some kind of freak.' But they are all sinners, too. Don't you see that nobody condemns you? You're not alone, lady."

A Word of Forgiveness

Jesus' second statement was one of *forgiveness.* "Neither do I condemn you" (John 8:11). As long as I feel that God holds my sins against me, I cannot grow. But when I am convinced that God harbors no grudge, I can breathe the fresh air of new beginnings.

A woman once told her minister that Jesus came to visit her nightly before she went to bed. The minister was understandably skeptical. He questioned such favored treatment from heaven, but the woman insisted that it really happened every night. So the preacher suggested a little test. "I committed a serious sin before entering the ministry. Ask Jesus tonight what that sin was and come back tomorrow with your answer. If you find out what the sin was, I will believe your story about personal visits from above."

The next day the dubious preacher asked, "Well, did you learn anything?"

"Yes. I asked Him," the woman explained, "but He said He doesn't remember sins already forgiven."

The totally humiliated woman standing before Jesus didn't need to be reminded of her sins. She was painfully aware of them. What she needed was healing. She needed to be reminded that permanent forgiveness was within arm's length, that with forgiveness comes forgetting.

James wrote an interesting prescription for the treatment and healing of sin. "Confess your sins to each other and pray for each other so that you may be healed" (James 5:16).

What does the word "healed" presuppose? That a wound exists. The result of sin is a wound, a deep, infected lesion that is in need of not the salt of accusation, but the soothing balm of forgiveness. Jesus wanted her to get it out, get it over—and then to get on with life.

In other words, "You are forgiven, too." What sweet-sounding words! I need those words often. We all do. We all harbor and hide our secrets and, at times, suffer alone. But this is so needless, when we could confess and be healed. His kind word for us can be, "I don't condemn you either. You're forgiven."

What if Jesus had said, "Well, I may not be smart, but I'm no dummy. If I'm going to continue My ministry I obviously can't afford to alienate the power structure. The salvation of the whole world is at stake. It's a tough decision, ma'am. I understand that you've got a problem here, but, you see, you're only one person and My ministry is bigger than that. Bring on the rocks, fellows. Sorry, lady."

Imbalance can abuse individual people in the name of a broader ministry. I've seen it happen. You, too, right? Now, I realize that institutions can't play favorites. But God's ministry flourishes through redemptive relationships, not through right policy. In God's system of things, people are "job one." It is *never right* to *do wrong* to a person in the name of a larger good. Never.

Did I hear someone say, "Well, I realize that this person is remorseful, but we've got to make an example of this case." Not with Jesus. When it comes to applying the Law of God, we ought to lean the way Jesus leaned: mercy, not sacrifice. Jesus definitely applied the Law of God to this woman's life. He said, "Don't sin anymore." But He also applied the will of God when He said, "You are forgiven." Mercy. God Himself says that people are always more valuable than principles and institutions.

Jesus' creative principle here: *Fight for people.* We are all infinitely precious to Him and to our Father. Of course, Jesus was a person of principle. Yet, He was even more willing to fight for people than to fight for principles. It is never right to do wrong by a person—never!

A Word of Healing

And how creatively He fights for her—and for them. First He offered *acceptance* in reminding her that she wasn't alone in her sins. Second, He offered *forgiveness* and a fresh start. But now He *demands change.* "Go now and leave your life of sin" (John 8:11). The reason He said this was not because He was trying to shore up the Law or protect the system; it was because He didn't want that woman to break herself. People were not made for promiscuous sex. And to use ourselves that way is as destructive as using a Stradivarius violin to drive tent pegs. Adultery wrecks intimacy. Adultery smashes self-esteem. Adultery destroys trust, and adultery not only is offensive in the eyes of God, but breaks God's heart!

Here is balance. You see, it would have been lopsided and incomplete for Jesus to offer the woman compassion with no challenge. For while she was clearly a pawn in the Pharisees' power play, she was also a sinner. She had chosen to surrender to her own lust. A loving Jesus couldn't ignore that.

It is never loving to pretend that there is no sin or that the sin doesn't matter because sin matters so tremendously.

A young boy received in the mail a record that he had ordered. When he opened the package he found that the company had failed to perforate a hole in the record. So the boy decided to make his own hole. It's not hard to guess what happened. The hole that the boy made was so off-center that the record swaggered and wobbled all over the turntable. And the sound? It was horrible.

That is exactly what happens when we ignore God's design for our lives and make up our own rules for the game. That is what the Bible calls sin! Sin operates life from self, not God, as the center. Jesus' advice to the woman caught in adultery was clear and compelling. "Don't sin any more. You are too valuable for that. You matter to God. You were made for more than that. So get your life back on the proper center, or there will be no harmony, no music inside you!"

What favor do we perform for wayward, searching friends if we don't call them to change? What kind of physician stitches a wound but then offers no medication or therapy? Does love offer acceptance and forgiveness and no rescue? As Paul the apostle put it, "Shall we go on sinning so that grace may increase? By no means!" (Rom. 6:1-2)

Remember? Balance! Here it is again: *Beware of a view of the law that harms people and a view of people that ignores sin.*

With Music in Her Ears

We don't know where this woman went from there. Scripture follows her no further. Some assume she became one of the faithful women who assisted Jesus in His ministry. Others even imagine she was present at the cross. It is possible, however, that she didn't take Jesus' advice. She may even have gone right back into the sack from which she had been yanked. Who knows?

We do know one thing for sure. She had heard the music of Jesus' orchestra. She wasn't bombarded with the relentless roar of a kettledrum. Nor was she fed only the sweet grace of the flute. No, the music she heard as directed by the master conductor was a symphony, a balance of compassion with correction.

Some of us "religious" people seem prone toward extremism or imbalance. The devil must take special delight in tipping Christians off-balance. Jesus loves balance even more than Satan hates it. If I will follow Jesus, I move to strike His balance and maintain it in all my dealings with people.

Focus:

1. What is spiritual balance to you?

2. Describe a situation where a view of the law may be harmful to people, then one where a view of people can make you ignore sin.
3. Have you been in a situation where God's Word was misapplied so that the growth of God's people did not occur? Describe it.
4. How is it possible to achieve balance in our spiritual lives?
5. How did Jesus offer the woman the correct balance of compassion with correction? How can you put His principles into your life?

Oh, no! Not this again. It's bad enough not being able to see. Why do some people have to humiliate blind people just for sport? Like, last week, some kids dumped the coins from my cup into the sand. Then when I bent down to scratch around and find them, those kids kicked dirt in my face and ran away laughing.

And the loud talkers. They seem to think that blind people are also deaf. They shout their greetings in my ear. Others say the most painful things, right out loud. Like the woman yesterday who stood right there and complained to her husband that the stuff running from my eye sockets turned her stomach.

So naturally I was suspicious when this gang of men walked up. I heard them ask the old questions again, right in front of me, as if I had no more feelings than a rock or a tree. "Is it his sin or that of his parents that took his sight?"

The unusual note in His voice encouraged me. I felt He was giving me dignity. And He said something about God. But then He did the most confusing thing. I can hear small noises, you know. So I heard the creak of His sandals and the rustle of His cloak as He knelt down. I could hear His fingers scratching around in the dirt. The rustle again as He stood. Then I hear Him hock saliva from His throat, and spit it in His hands. Next I was sure I could hear a squishy sound, like He was making spit-mud in His hand.

Then came the shock. Splat! He smacked His handful of spit-mud right in one of my eyes. This had to be the dirtiest trick anyone pulled on me yet. I didn't know what to do. I wanted to run. Yet I held my ground, hoping they would leave. Then He repeated the process—splat—in my other eye!

Double insult. Finally He ordered, "Go wash your face in the pool!"

Here was my chance at an exit! So I picked up my stick and tapped off in the direction of Siloam. When I felt my stick splash the water, I fell on my knees and scooped handfuls of water onto my face and into my eyes until I heard my tormenters leave.

But then, when I stood up, for the first time in my life I saw light. Then trees. Water. Sky. Birds. Flowers.

I dropped my stick and ran for home . . . and chaos!

10

Beware of Labels

One of our sons-in-law, Wes, is a musician. He and our daughter moved to Colorado Springs on their wedding day ten years ago. They both love the mountains, and Wes had bookings in that area. They quickly found an apartment and left a résumé, a check, and a verbal agreement. But when they called to pick up a key, the manager back-peddled, "Well, I'm having second thoughts. I noticed that you are a musician. Sorry, but we can't accept your application because our company caters to the more stable type of tenant."

Wes is an unusually even-tempered guy, but that got him steamed. He's never left

Pigeon-holing People into Convenient Categories

a bill unpaid. He doesn't drink. He doesn't smoke. He doesn't like loud music. He doesn't throw wild parties, and he especially doesn't like being labeled as "unstable" because he is a musician.

Actually Wes is like all the rest of us. We like to be who we are. We want to be treated like people, not like categories. Jesus underscores this as He encounters a special person in the ninth chapter of John. Watch Him in action!

"As he went along, he saw a man blind from birth" (John 9:1). That's availability. Jesus gave him sight. That's helpfulness.

They Could Not See What They Would Not See

But the healing of this blind man triggered a barrage of questions from every direction. The disciples of Jesus didn't understand, nor did the blind man's family or the neighbors. And the Pharisees surely didn't understand. The whole thing created such an uproar that the poor fellow got kicked out of his own church. However, the biggest blindness was in the minds of the people who raised questions about the man whom Jesus healed. They couldn't see the man, the human being who was given eyesight. They only saw labels. But trace Jesus' movements through this whole experience, and we'll learn some creative people-sensitivity.

A Question

First, the disciples asked Jesus, "Rabbi, who sinned, this man or his parents, that he was born blind?" (John 9:2) A logical question. For centuries tradition said that people were struck by catastrophe because of sin, either theirs or their parents'.

But the disciples failed to see the person beyond the *religious question*. What a convenient way to dismiss persons: quite creative, when you stop and think about it. Just head off into a world of abstractions, and you never have to actually deal with real people. And you can feel justified, too, because the abstractions are *religious* ones. While the abstract discussion continued, the blind man's feelings were ignored.

I saw something like this happen. A person who had undergone a sex-change operation years earlier began attending our church. No one in the church knew this person's secret past. One Sunday, while this person sat in Bible class, the group launched into a lively debate about sex-change surgery and Christian ethics. Let me tell you, if you want discussion that will occupy religious people for a while, that question has infinite possibilities. Why, you can cite experts on surgery, on sex, on morality, on theology, even on psychology; you can analyze the issue from now till Judgment morning. You may hit the speakers' circuit with a seminar on "Sex Change and the Christian" and *never actually* even know a real live person who has had a sex-change surgery . . . much less offer Christ's compassion. I listened and watched that Sunday morning as the sex-changed person felt like a "thing"—no, more like a category.

Another time I recall sitting in a church office heatedly discussing whether or not Christians should attempt to help "druggies while they were actually stoned." Then we walked out of the church to find a teenage girl lying unconscious on the sidewalk in the hot sun. She was toxified on drugs, had passed out, and was nearly dead—*right in front of the church*—while we sat inside exploring drug abusers as abstract religious questions!

A Category

Second, the blind man's neighbors took a similar tack. They asked, "Isn't this the beggar?" *The neighbors saw a label*; to them he was not a person, but "the beggar." Someone said, "Labels are libels." "He's a musician! Not in our apartment!" Labeling smoothly and conveniently distances us from involvement and dehumanizes the person getting labeled. Yet, paradoxically, at the time we slap on the label, we may even feel that we have "handled" the person because we understand what "category" he or she belongs to.

"Oh, Tom? He's an alcoholic."

Excuse me. I'm sorry. I treated him like a person.

"See that guy over there? He's gay."

So? Should that change my basic way of treating him? Because his sin is homosexuality, does that make him less than a person?

"Susan? You know, she's a hooker."

Oh, I thought she was a human being. Maybe we need to get closer to Susan, a person who matters to God, to love her with Christ's love.

"Jim is radical, right-wing, ultra-conservative (or was it left wing, ultra-liberal?). Let me out of here. Give me air."

"Sarah is a divorcée!" (We usually don't say that person *was* divorced or has *been* divorced or even *used to be married*. It's easier to say "a divorcée.")

Categories! Bam, stick on the label! Cover up the person. Sidestep involvement and relationship.

One "Christian" door-knocking crusader instructed each participant, "As quickly as possible, find out if the people in that home have been previously married. If so, exit as quickly and gracefully as you can and go talk to somebody who is not damaged goods."

Can you imagine Jesus reacting to the Samaritan woman that way? "Oh, My goodness. Well, I'd better exit this conversation. Maybe there's another well down the road somewhere with a better woman sitting by it. Can't waste any more time here."

A Problem

Then, the *Pharisees* viewed the blind man from a third perspective. "The day on which Jesus had made the mud and opened the man's eyes was a Sabbath" (John 9:14)—bingo! Sabbath! First clue something's gone wrong.

"Tell us how you received your sight."

"[Jesus] put mud on my eyes . . . and I washed, and now I see" (John 9:15).

"Aha! We've got a problem here. This healer is not from God or He wouldn't do this on the Sabbath."

The Pharisees saw a problem! Not a person! "We've got to discredit this 'healer' of blind men. If our people go off after Him, we'll lose our power. We'll have problems. We must keep our religious forum at all costs, even if we have to dump blind men out of the church. After all, our forum has been around a lot longer than this guy has."

The Pharisees had ignored the big question Jesus asked on a previous occasion when He had been criticized for Sabbath-day healing, "Which is lawful on the Sabbath: to do good or to do evil, to save life or to destroy it?" (Luke 6:9)

They hadn't responded because they really weren't interested in the Sabbath law, nor in doing good. All they wanted was to protect their power at whatever people-cost. In Jesus' day, or ours, whenever religious institutional force is used to crush human beings, then God's purposes are being prostituted.

We as God's people cannot let any institutional or political agenda distract us from Christ-like respect and compassion for individual persons. When we abuse persons for *any* reason, we're doing dreadful wrong. When we abuse persons in the name of God, we're damaging the very nerve center of our faith. What could be a more destructive evil than toxic religion, which downgrades the value and meaning of persons?

A Role

A fourth perspective on this blind man came from his *parents*. The parents were frightened. Some people got kicked out of the synagogue for crossing swords with the leaders. And a sure way to offend the leaders was to admit interest in Jesus.

"Is this your son?" the leaders asked. "How is it that he can now see?"

"Yes, he's our son all right. Yes, he was born blind and can now see! But, no, we don't know who opened his eyes or how it was done!"

The parents' view is self-protective. Distortions of truth usually are. "This is our son; he is our biological offspring." *They saw their son in a "role," not as an autonomous, precious person.*

God pity the son and daughter whose parents see them only as "our kids"; and heartbreak may be ahead for the mother or father whose children see them as "my old man" and "my old lady." Respect is on the way out of a marriage when a spouse sneers, "Oh, that's only my husband (or wife) talking." This domestic discounting is incredibly easy to do to the people who are closest. Believe me, I know; I've done it.

What Jesus Saw

Finally, notice Jesus' view of the blind man. Pick up the story at the beginning. Jesus *saw a man, blind from birth.* That's *sensitivity.* A world of loneliness and helplessness is packed into that phrase! Each word carries special poignancy. "*Saw!*" "*Blind!*" "Saw a *man!*" "Blind *all of his life!*"

Still today blindness dehumanizes, but much more so in Jesus' day. Left begging. Avoided. Ridiculed. Ostracized as a sure sinner, under a curse! When Jesus *saw* the person, He sensed all these things. Jesus saw this person! Jesus also saw an opportunity for God! He said, "This happened so that the work of God might be displayed in his life" (John 9:3).

Every human being holds potential to reveal God's marvelous glory. In fact, John said that although no human eye will physically see God, yet "If we love each other, God lives in us and his love is made complete in us" (1 John 4:12).

A 1980s TV commercial comes to mind: A little boy stared hungrily into the bakery window. He wore ragged clothes and had no money. "Mean Joe Green," a former Pittsburgh Steeler Pro-Bowler, spotted the little guy, edged up alongside him, and asked, "Do you like those doughnuts?"

"Yeah."

The little boy didn't know Mean Joe. Didn't even look at him. Joe went inside while the little boy, waiting for Joe, pressed his nose against the window. When Joe came out, he stuffed a sackful of hot doughnuts into the little fellow's arms. The scene faded as the little guy looked toward the camera and asked, "Was that man God?"

Jesus said, "As long as it is day, we must do the work of him who sent me." How? By treating people like *people*. We are meant to reflect the gentleness of God, the kindness of God, the goodness, the mercy, the patience, the joy, the peace, the courage, and sensitivity of God. And be creatively personal—like God. Then the work of God is being done. Through us! Then people can see God in us!

I am prone to become so task-oriented that I make little time for people. I rationalize that the task is "the work of God." But God's work is *people*. When we're doing right by people, we're doing the work of God—in the office, at home, down at the service station, at the gym. When God's work enriches our relationships, *folks see God.*

Several years ago in Arkansas a non-church-going lady was befriended by some people in a small town church. Her baby fell sick with a life-threatening illness that lasted for weeks. People from that church took turns holding the baby, day and night, around the clock. They cleaned her house, put food in the refrigerator, even helped pay the medical bills.

The lady began attending that church. Her non-churched friends asked, "Are you going to church somewhere?"

"Yes."

"Oh, watch out for churches. They are full of 'goody-goodies.' They only want your money. They say that everybody is going to go to hell but them."

The lady responded, "I've never heard them say that, and I've been over there for weeks. I only know that when I thought my baby was dying, *they held my baby.*"

Sounds a lot like, "I just know that I was blind, and now I can see." The world's most profound and eloquent preaching can't touch people nearly so deeply as will the love of God in human skin.

When the blind man was healed, the crowd saw a religious question, a label, a problem, a role. But none of them saw him as a *person*. Only Jesus saw the man.

What the Blind Man Saw

Let's walk through the story once again, this time in the blind man's shoes: A group of strangers pops up. He's probably run into this a thousand times. "Oh, go on, don't bug me. Don't humiliate me more. What's your trick? Don't steal my pencils, or take the money out of my tin cup. What's going on?"

Then the stranger rubs spit-mud into the man's eyes and tells him to go to the pool.

The blind man endured the spit. Splat! He was probably steeled against that kind of thing. Likely a lot of dirtier tricks had been pulled on him through the years. So he headed for the pool, splashed water in his eyes, and shouted "Hallelujah, I can see!"

Give Me Space

Let's move further into the blind man's psyche. Jesus had focused, not on His own *agenda*, but on the blind man's *need*. I really need to learn that. Our human tendency is to make people beholden, to hook them so we can swing them into our agenda. But Jesus is neither pushy nor manipulative. He just meets the man's needs, then gives him space. None of us likes to be shoved into things, even good things.

I heard the story about a soldier who spotted a blind man being jostled by the crowd at the airport. The blind man had dropped his white cane and was trying to retrieve it so he could cross to another part of the terminal. The soldier stopped and offered, "Sir, can I help you?" The blind man beamed his appreciation, "Yes, could you help me cross the street?" The soldier himself was nearly late for his flight, but he picked up the cane, put it in the blind man's hand, then grabbed the blind man's arm and hurriedly shoved him across the street. The poor fellow shrugged the soldier loose and protested, "Don't push me, man. Don't possess me! I just need your touch on my shoulder to guide me where I'm going."

Jesus was just that gentle with His touch for this blind man in the Bible. Jesus still doesn't shove people around, nor should we.

Of course, for this blind man, as for all of us, the central need was for God. That is the need Jesus aimed to meet. But Jesus chose good timing. He didn't open the conversation with the central need. First off, Jesus met the man's felt need: He gave him sight. No strings attached and no manipulation. But this opened the way for something bigger. Things began changing inside the person. When a human need is met in such a way, the work of God is begun.

Jesus sent the man to the pool where he would find sight. Then Jesus *left*! He left so unobtrusively that the Bible doesn't even record Jesus' absence till later on.

No Strings Attached

What Jesus did is unique. It would be reasonably safe to say that not one person in a hundred thousand experiences something being done for him with *absolutely no strings attached!* None!

Jesus just healed and hurried away. He left no calling card. He sent no bill. Took down no names. He collected no tips. He didn't even explain Himself! That's pretty unique, isn't it?

When you stop and think about it, that's exactly what He's doing with us. No strings. Just meets our needs. When they put Him on a cross, He didn't bargain, "Father, if You'll guarantee Me ten thousand converts in the first five years, I'll go through with this." No guarantees. He just died—that's all.

When most of us help people, there are strings! Of course, we attempt to hide them, even from ourselves. But we usually expect something out of it when we help people. At the very least, we want to make them feel obligated to listen when we witness to them. But people aren't stupid, especially people who have lived a long time in the darkness, being misused and manipulated and pushed around by nearly everybody. They can feel a string a mile off, even if it's only psychological. Can smell it coming. We all expect strings.

My friend Landon Saunders tells of a conversation someone overheard in the ladies' room during break at one of his seminars. "What's the catch here? Do you suppose these things he's giving away are really free?" Another lady said, "I think I've got it figured out. They are free to us; but he's going to want us to sell them to our neighbors." They expected strings, couldn't believe anything could really be free.

To treat people like Jesus treats people is to help with no strings attached. When a person is genuinely treated the way God would treat him, the action won't go ignored. It is fed into that person's spiritual software. Once there, it may gestate a long time, but it's still working.

What Jesus did "worked" on the blind man. He had to deal with the internal processes going on inside his own soul. "I can see again. I don't understand why. It's upsetting the neighborhood terribly. Even friends of the healer are asking critical questions. My parents are scared to death. But I sure do like seeing."

Spiritual Gestation

The blind man needed space and time to process his experience. He had to struggle very personally and privately with the implications of it all.

First, he may have wondered, "What is the catch? When does the other shoe fall? What does the healer expect out of this?" Then he may have reflected further, "But I can *see*. A blind man receives his sight! That's pretty amazing. I can't ignore something this big! Now, the Pharisees are saying the man who gave me sight is a sinner. But if that's true, how could He have healed me? Who is the man?"

Pressure came from every direction. When testing comes, no one can help us escape the test. Testing comes in the naked loneliness of the soul. No one can shove us through, like the soldier tried to shove the blind man through the airport.

Jesus didn't shove this man, but other people kept after him till finally the man said, "He is a prophet" (John 9:17b). The Pharisees went ballistic!

"Prophet?!"

"Yes, I think He's a prophet."

The Pharisees summoned the man who had been healed. A "summons" is serious stuff. I picture the Pharisees around a horseshoe-shaped table with the man who had been blind on a chair in the middle. "Give glory to God," they demanded (John 9:24). What do you do with that? Their demand only led the man to probe deeper into the implications of his amazing experience. Notice: During this debate, Jesus didn't sit at the man's elbow or pass him notes. He left the man alone.

"We know this man is a sinner."

"All I know is that I used to be blind and now I can see."

Then they demanded, "How did your 'healer' do this?"

Read: "Some kind of mumbo jumbo? Black magic? Snake oil?" "I told you *once*," the man replied. "Why do you want to hear it *again*?"

Point of No Return

His mind was edging slowly but surely toward the point of no return. He is now approaching ground zero! Decision time. The questioners inadvertently guide him toward that decision. But Jesus didn't push him, whispering, "Come on, come on," though the man may have been whispering that to himself.

Then the man stepped across the line. He finally blurted out, "Do you want to become His disciples . . . *too*?" By adding the word "too" he implied, "Like me! Yes. I am already a disciple." Decision! He had finally moved that far.

This was too much for the Pharisees. "You are this fellow's disciple? We're disciples of Moses. Who knows where this Jesus guy came from?"

Don't miss the next line. It is both salt in their wounds and nails in his coffin: "Well, that's remarkable. I thought you guys were theologians! Jesus opened my eyes! Yet you don't know where He's from? Come, come. What have you been teaching me in Sabbath school all these years? You taught me that God doesn't listen to sinners. Right? He only listens to the godly man. Now, nobody, but *nobody* has ever heard of opening the eyes of a man born blind. Why, gentlemen, if this man weren't from God, He could do nothing of this magnitude!"

Retrace this man's emerging commitment. "I don't know." "I think He's a prophet." "I am His disciple." *"This man is from God."*

With that, the Pharisees exploded! "You are steeped in sin. Blind, right? The result of sin! Where do you get the nerve to lecture us on theology?" When they had verbally unloaded on him, they threw him out of the synagogue.

What a turbulent day it was for this man. Absolutely confusing. He gets eyesight in the morning. Then the world goes crazy. By mid-afternoon, he lands on his head in the dust outside the synagogue, feeling like a quarterback sacked by a 300-pound linebacker. Did he wonder, "Maybe being able to see isn't such a good thing after all"? But he's made his decision.

Jesus gave space. Waited. Jesus didn't breathe down this man's neck. Didn't harass. Let him think things through. He respected the struggle going on in this man's soul. Yet God has been drawing him, gently tugging at the man's heart!

In a sixty-minute conversation with a stranger on an aircraft, we need not strain to swing the topic around to religion. Jesus wouldn't operate like that. He didn't Rolodex names for follow-up. When we treat a person "Jesus style," we need not push him or her to do everything at once. God has another messenger stationed somewhere down the road to pick up where we left off. We never serve uselessly. God stations His witnesses where He wants them. Through them, He sets up the work of His Spirit on that heart. God is drawing, still. Some will respond positively. But most won't. Not even for Jesus. That's a good thing to remember. Leaves us at peace.

180 / Heaven Came Down

Consolidating Gains

When Jesus heard the man had been thrown out of the synagogue, He found the man and asked, "Do you believe in Me?" Why did Jesus wait till now to ask this question? What if Jesus had pressed the question at His first encounter with the blind man, "Hey, Mr. Blind Man. Can you hear me? I know you can't see. But can you hear me?"

"Yes, I can hear just fine."

"Okay, then listen. You need to believe that I am the Messiah."

"It's my eyes, my eyes. Do you know what it's like to be blind? It's my eyes, 'Messiah.' If you want to help me, help me where I hurt. Help me see!"

But, of course, that's not how Jesus began. He began with the eyes, precisely where the man hurt. Jesus gave him sight, then backed off to give him space, dignity, and personhood.

But now Jesus steps back into the picture because He sees the man is ready for the big question: "Do you believe in the Messiah?" inquired Jesus.

"Who is He, sir, so that I can believe in Him?" This man has never seen Jesus before. On the last encounter with Jesus, the man was still blind. So, of course, he did not recognize Jesus by sight. It did not occur to him at that point that he was actually standing face to face with the Messiah. Even as I write these words, I feel goosebumps up my spine. What a moment! All of the angels must have held their breath, straining forward, watching! Jesus very quietly says, "The Messiah is talking to you." Wham!

Suddenly, everything fits. The man burst out, "I believe," and he worshiped Jesus. Then all the angels must have burst into "The Hallelujah Chorus"! This man had finally arrived at his moment of commitment by an internal process that began much earlier with "no strings attached" service.

And so it is that Jesus commissions us to treat people in this same way. Discern needs. Do what we can. Then back off. But don't go too far away. Watch with loving eyes as God works in them. Pray. Wait for the time when they're ready for the next step toward God. Then be there when the time is right.

Focus:

1. When is a time you were labeled? How did it feel?
2. Why do we feel secure in labeling?
3. What are some ways you can overcome labeling in your church?

Epilogue

E. H. Ijams lived more than ninety years and died over a decade ago. Twenty years ago I heard him tell of a special Sunday afternoon when he was a young man in Nashville, Tennessee. He had often been invited to speak Sunday afternoons to a congregation in the inner city. One afternoon, he said, "I read my text, 'Have this mind among yourselves that you have in Christ Jesus.' As I laid my Bible aside and drew a breath to begin the sermon, a little boy sitting near the back began singing, softly at first, in a thin voice, 'I wanta' be like Jesus, in my heart.' Soon another voice, chimed in, 'wanta' be like Jesus in my heart.' Then one by one, till everyone in the room joined the chorus and that old building shook and throbbed, 'I want to be like Jesus in my heart.'"

That *is* what I want to be. How about you? To be like Jesus in our hearts: available, sensitive, helpful, and creative—as creative as the uniqueness of each person God is pleased to touch through us.

Notes

1. Alan Loy McGinnis, *The Friendship Factor* (Minneapolis: Augsburg, 1979), 15.
2. Clyde E. Fant, Jr. and William M. Pinson, Jr., *Twenty Centuries of Great Preaching, Volume 6, Spurgeon to Meyer, 1834-1929* (Waco, Texas: Word, 1971), 31.
3. M.D. Gibson, *Horae Semiticae* (Cambridge, 1913), 40.
4. George Barna, *The Frog in the Kettle* (Ventura, California: Regal Books, 1990), 117, 119.
5. Jim Dethmer, "The Unchurched: Understanding Them to Reach Them," *The Pastor's Update*, Charles E. Fuller Institute of Evangelism and Church Growth, Pasadena, California. Tape # U009204, April 1992.
6. Stephen B. Oates, *With Malice Toward None* (New York: Harper & Row Publishers, 1977), 412.
7. Taken from *The Singer* by Calvin Miller. © 1975 by InterVarsity Christian Fellowship of the USA. Used by permission of InterVarsity Press, P.O. Box 1400, Downers Grove, IL 60515.
8. George MacLeod, *Only One Way Left* (Glasgow: The Iona Community, 1956), 38.
9. William Glasser, *Reality Therapy* (New York: Harper & Row Publishers, 1965), 93-94.
10. Roger S. Greenway and Timothy M. Monsma, *Cities: Mission's New Frontier* (Grand Rapids: Baker Books, 1989), 51, 53.
11. Viktor E. Frankl, *Man's Search for Meaning*, revised and updated, translation by Ilse Lasch (Boston: Washington Square Press, 1959), 12.
12. Bill Hybels, "Discovering How God Wired You Up," Seeds Tape M91151-0407, Part 1, Temperament.
13. Don McLeese's review of Nick Tosche's *Dino: Living High in the Dirty Business of Dreams, Dallas Morning News*, September 1, 1992, 3.
14. Paul Burka, "Honesty is the Best Politics," *Texas Monthly*, November 1992, 122-25, 156.
15. James E. Dittes, *When the People Say No* (New York: Harper & Row Publishers, 1979), 2, 4-5.

About the Author

Lynn spent eleven years planting churches in Canada before he became minister of the Highland Church of Christ in Abilene, Texas, for nineteen years. In 1990, he took a writing sabbatical, completing three books, and travelled extensively. He spoke in a different pulpit each Sunday including pulpits in Ethiopia, Canada, and Mexico. He became pulpit minister of the Preston Road Church of Christ in Dallas in October 1991.

Lynn is the author of *Finding the Heart to Go On* (Here's Life), *Freshness for the Far Journey* (ACU Press), and *If I Really Believe, Why Do I Have These Doubts?* (Bethany Press).

He and his wife, Carolyn, have four grown children and seven grandchildren. Lynn has his BA and MA from Harding University and his Doctorate from Abilene Christian University.